W9-BWI-945

CHRÉTIEN de TROYES

YWAIN
The Knight of the Lion

Translated by
ROBERT W. ACKERMAN
Stanford University

FREDERICK W. LOCKE
Stanford University

CARLETON W. CARROLL
Oregon State University

Complete Edition

FREDERICK UNGAR PUBLISHING CO.
NEW YORK

MILESTONES OF THOUGHT
in the History of Ideas

Library of Congress Cataloging in Publication Data

Chrestien de Troyes, 12th cent.
  Ywain, the knight of the lion.

  (Milestones of thought)
  Translation of Chevalier au lyon.
  Bibliography: p.
  1. Ywain—Romances. I. Ackerman, Robert William, 1910—
II. Locke, Frederick W. III. Carroll, Carleton W. IV. Title. V.
Series: Milestones of thought in the history of ideas.
PQ1447.E5A2   1977   841'.1   77-10461
ISBN 0-8044-6084-1

INTRODUCTION

THE TWELFTH century in Europe witnessed a great awakening, an anticipation of the high Renaissance of the fifteenth century. In France, one of the most notable aspects of this early movement was the flowering of vernacular literature, especially the troubadour poetry of the south and the somewhat later narrative literature, the court epic or romance.

The most talented of the writers of romance was Chrétien de Troyes, a native of the county of Champagne in northern France, who seems to have written his poems for courtly circles during the period 1160–1180. His *Lancelot,* for example, was composed at the behest of Countess Marie of Champagne, daughter of one of the most remarkable of all mediaeval women, Eleanor of Aquitaine, and his *Perceval* was dedicated to Count Philip of Flanders. We know that Chrétien wrote at least seven romances, of which five, including *Yvain,* are preserved, and also a number of translations and reworkings of Latin poems, chiefly Ovidian.

Yvain, or *Ywain,* as the name of the title character is anglicized here, is thought to have been written between 1169 and 1173. The principal characters and episodes of this story, as of Chrétien's other Arthurian romances, are Celtic in origin, in the opinion of most recent scholars. Ywain, the son of Urien, for example, may well have got his name from an historical Briton of the sixth century. The adventures assigned to the hero, however, such as his encounter with the Wild Man of the forest, his experience at the marvelous spring, and his befriending of the lion, were apparently derived from Celtic story lore. It is entirely possible that the outlines at least of the tale of Ywain, as well as of other Arthurian stories, reached Chrétien through the medium of Breton *conteurs* who were ultimately indebted to insular traditions.

Like Shakespeare, then, Chrétien achieved greatness not by plot innovation so much as by shaping existing and perhaps widely known material to his own purposes. We will never know the exact nature of his sources, of course, but we can nonetheless say something about the poet's personal contributions to his romances. For one thing, Chrétien's four Arthurian poems tend to fall into a fairly distinctive pattern. The opening scene is laid in Arthur's court where, amidst the imposing nobles of the Round Table, an untried young man is presented with a challenge. Upon accepting, he sets out alone and, after surmounting many perils and winning many combats, he performs the appointed labor and, by way of reward, receives a wife and vast estate, as does Ywain. But almost immediately, he is made aware of some shortcoming in himself, and he promptly abandons his happiness to undertake a second quest the object of which is to expiate or repair the fault. This series of adventures is concluded by a joyous reunion with the lady and occasionally with Arthur's court as well. Because Chrétien convinces us that the hero's later experiences bring him to a higher pitch of self-knowledge than he had attained heretofore, we accept the reunion as final and enduring, as a true fulfillment. In particular, Ywain's moral regeneration during his second course of exploits is signalized by his selfless rescue of the lion from the clutches of the dragon and by his assumption of the sobriquet, the Knight of the Lion.

The flow of Chrétien's octosyllabic couplets lends an appropriately urbane expression to his narratives, imbued as they are with the ideals and sentiments of courtly knighthood. It is true that the leisurely, elevated conversation of the characters often strikes us as needlessly repetitious and the extended metaphors, in terms of which Chrétien in his own person sometimes analyzes motives and feelings, as prolix in the extreme. An obvious example of the latter tendency occurs when Ywain takes leave of his bride in order to go tourneying with Gawain. King Arthur, we are told, is able to lead away the hero's body but not his heart, for it is too firmly in Laudine's possession. Normally, a body may not live on without a heart, but Ywain is enabled to maintain life by fashioning a new heart out of hope. It is interesting to note that metaphorical flights of this sort are omitted in the Middle English translation and that in consequence the two poems differ markedly in total effect.

A reading of Chrétien's several narrative poems suffices to demonstrate that his influence on the characteristic structure, tone, and theme of mediaeval romance was very great. Of his romances, *Ywain* has most often been singled out as the highest expression of his art. Morever, *Ywain* was paid the homage of imitation by a number of mediaeval writers, including Hartmann von Aue and an accomplished, if anonymous English poet of the fourteenth century.

ROBERT W. ACKERMAN

FREDERICK W. LOCKE

EDITIONS AND TRANSLATIONS

Yvain (*Der Löwenritter*), ed. Wendelin Foerster. 4th revised ed. Halle: Max Niemeyer, 1912. (Romanische Bibliothek, No. 5); reprinted Geneva: Slatkine Reprints, 1977.

Arthurian Romances, translated by W. Wistar Comfort, with an introduction and notes by D. D. R. Owen. London: J. M. Dent and Sons, Ltd., 1975, pp. 180–269. (Everyman's Library Nos. 698, hardback, and 1698, paperback.) This translation was first published in 1914.

Yvain, ou Le Chevalier au Lion, translated into modern French by André Mary; introduction and notes by Julian Harris. New York: Dell Publishing Co., Inc., 1963. This translation was originally published in Paris: Gallimard, 1925.

Yvain (*Le Chevalier au lion*): the critical text of Wendelin Foerster, with introduction, notes and glossary by T. B. W. Reid. Manchester: The University Press, 1942; reprinted 1948.

Yvain, übersetzt und eingeleitet von Ilse Nolting-Hauff. München: Eidos Verlag, 1962. (Klassische Texte des Romanischen Mittelalters in zweisprachigen Ausgaben.) Bilingual edition, German and Old French, following Foerster's 4th edition.

Le Chevalier au lion (*Yvain*), publié par Mario Roques. Paris: Librairie Ancienne Honoré Champion, 1963. (Les Classiques Français du Moyen Age, No. 89). This constitutes volume IV of Les Romans de Chrétien de Troyes édités d'après la copie de Guiot (Bibl. nat. fr. 794).

Yvain ou Le Chevalier au Lion, préparé par Jan Nelson [et]

Carleton W. Carroll, avec une introduction par Douglas Kelly. New York: Appleton-Century-Crofts, 1968.

Yvain ou le chevalier au lion, extraits: traduction en français moderne . . . par André Eskénazi. Paris: Librairie Larousse, 1970.

Le Chevalier au lion (*Yvain*), roman traduit de l'ancien français par Claude Buridant et Jean Trotin. Paris: Librairie Honoré Champion, 1974.

Yvain or the Knight with the Lion, translated by Ruth Harwood Cline, with a foreword by Julian Harris. Athens (Georgia): The University of Georgia Press, 1975. Verse translation, in octosyllabic couplets.

GENERAL STUDIES

Frappier, Jean. *Chrétien de Troyes, l'homme et l'œuvre.* Paris: Hatier, 1957; nouvelle édition 1968.

Loomis, Roger Sherman. *Arthurian Tradition and Chrétien de Troyes.* New York: Columbia University Press, 1949.

Several of the above-mentioned editions and both of the general studies contain extensive bibliographies. For references to the most recent publications relating to Chrétien and *Yvain*, consult the *Bibliographical Bulletin of the International Arthurian Society*, eds. Lewis Thorpe and Kenneth Varty.

NOTE ON THE TRANSLATION

WHEN PROFESSORS ACKERMAN AND LOCKE prepared their partial translation of *Ywain*, first published in 1957, they used the most readily accessible edition of Chrétien's poem available at that time, namely, the photographic reproduction of Foerster's 1912 revision of his earlier critical edition, first published in 1887, and republished with English-language introduction, notes, and glossary by T. B. W. Reid in 1942 and reprinted in 1948.[1] Since that time several other editions and translations of the romance have appeared, and in translating the portion of the text that Ackerman and Locke gave in summary form (corresponding to lines 3416-6526 of Foerster's edition) I have been guided by the work of some of these other scholars, in particular André Eskénazi's translation/edition for the Nouveaux Classiques Larousse series, Claude Buridant and Jean Trotin's translation, and by my own experience in helping to prepare the 1968 Appleton-Century-Crofts Old French edition. All three of these presentations were based primarily on the Guiot copy of the manuscript (Paris, Bibliothèque nationale, ms. fr. 794); a close comparison between my translation of these passages and the text as presented by Foerster would therefore reveal some (generally minor) discrepancies, since Foerster based his edition on two manuscripts, the Guiot copy and also B. nat. 1433, while consulting in addition all the other manuscripts of *Yvain* that were known in his day—a procedure that resulted in a composite text of the poem.

---

[1] See "Editions and Translations," page ix.

My aim in translating Chrétien's text has always been, as it was for Ackerman and Locke, "to render the sense of every passage as accurately as possible." In doing so, I have endeavored to avoid both archaic-sounding English and the overly modern idiom, the ideal being a style and a vocabulary that read smoothly and naturally and are thus readily accessible to readers of contemporary American/English prose. I have departed as little as possible from Chrétien's text. The main instances in which departure has been systematic involve, on the one hand, the tense of narration (uniformly set in the past, instead of varying between past and present, as in the original), and, on the other, the introduction of names or nouns, to replace pronouns when ambiguity seemed likely to occur. One of the peculiarities of Chrétien's style is his seeming reluctance to name some of his characters: the lady Ywain marries is named but once in the entire poem, although she is a major character and is referred to (primarily by the noun *dame*, "lady") at least 144 times; the damsel in her service first appears on page 17 of our translation, but it is only on page 41 that we learn that her name is Lunete; the two daughters of the lord of the Black Thorn, who appear many times in the last third of the romance, are never given names by Chrétien: instead he refers to them as "the elder sister" and "the younger sister" or, worse (from the standpoint of clarity), simply by pronouns (all the equivalent of "she") or as "the one" and "the other." While Chrétien's readers and listeners may not have been bothered by such stylistic devices, the modern reader is likely to be, and so the present translation attempts to avoid that particular difficulty.

Explanatory notes have been kept to a minimum, in order to interrupt the flow of the narrative as little as possible. Definitions of any additional unfamiliar words can be found in a good English dictionary.

CARLETON W. CARROLL

July, 1977

Chrétien de Troyes

YWAIN, THE KNIGHT OF THE LION

THE GOOD King Arthur of Britain, whose knighthood inspires us to be valiant and courteous, held a noble court as befits a king on that lavish feast day which men are accustomed to call Pentecost. The King was then at Carduel in Wales.

Having dined in the hall, the knights gathered at the invitation of the ladies and damsels. Some of them told adventure stories and others spoke about love, its pangs and sorrows and also its joys, which are the lot of the disciples of the order of love, still at that time vigorous and honorable even though it has few followers nowadays. Indeed, nearly all have abandoned it with the result that love is in very ill repute. Those who in the past obeyed the dictates of love were accounted valiant, generous, and worthy, but now love is turned into a trifling thing. Those who know nothing about it claim that they love, but they lie and make it a mockery and a deception. People who boast about love have no right to it.

But, if we are to speak about those who lived in days gone by, let us leave off talking about the present, for, in my opinion, better a courteous man even though dead than a live boor. Thus, I would like to tell a story which is worth the hearing about a king of such renown that men far and near still speak of him. For I agree wholly with the Bretons that his name will live for all time. And in connection with this king one recalls those good, picked knights who wrought great deeds of honor. On this Pentecost, the knights marveled

1

greatly at the King when he rose and departed from them. Some were much aggrieved and they discussed the matter at length. Never before at so great a feast had they seen the King enter his bower for sleep or rest. But on this occasion it happened that the Queen detained him, and he tarried so long beside her that he forgot himself and fell asleep.

Outside the door of the bower were Dodinel, Sagramore, Kay, my Lord Gawain, and Ywain. With them was also Calogrenant, a most worthy knight, who recounted an experience which brought not honor to him but rather disgrace. As he told his tale, the Queen heard him and, rising from the King's side, came upon the knights so unexpectedly that no one observed her approach. Only Calogrenant jumped up without delay. Thereupon Kay, who was most disagreeable, difficult, sharp-tongued, and insulting, said, "God bear me witness, Calogrenant! I see that you are very gallant and alert, and indeed, it is gratifying to me that you are the most courteous man of us all, and I know that you believe it of yourself, lacking as you are in good sense. It is only reasonable that my lady presume that you are better than the rest of us with respect to knightly courtesy and valor. It must seem that we neglected to stand out of laziness or because we did not choose to do so. But, by my faith, Sir, we in fact acted thus only because we did not see my lady until after you had arisen!"

"Indeed, Kay!" said the Queen, "in my opinion, you would certainly explode if you could not spew forth the venom you are so full of. You are tedious and ill-bred to quarrel with your comrades."

"My Lady," replied Kay, "even if we are not to improve by your presence, see that we do not lose thereby. I do not believe I have said anything that may be considered objectionable, and I beg you to speak no more about it. There is neither courtesy nor reason in continuing a meaningless quibble. This discussion ought not to go on further nor ought one to enlarge on it any more. But now, request him to relate

2

to us the tale he had begun since there is to be no contention."

Calogrenant then replied: "Sir," said he, "I do not feel any great concern about the argument. To me it is trifling and of small consequence. If you are scornful of me, I have suffered no harm from it. My Lord Kay, you have frequently offered insults to men more valiant and wise than I, for that is your nature. The dung heap will always stink and flies sting and bees hum, and the ill-tempered man will torment and vex others. But I will not tell my story today, if my lady will excuse me, and I beg that she be silent about a matter which is unpleasant to me and graciously excuse me from going on with it."

"Lady," said Kay, "all those present would be grateful to you because they would like to hear the story. But do not do anything for my sake. Rather, by the faith which you owe the King, your lord and mine, command him to tell his tale and you will act properly."

"Calogrenant," said the Queen, "do not mind this attack by my Lord Kay, the Seneschal. He is so accustomed to speak scurrilously that one cannot punish him. I beg of you not to be angered to the heart nor fail on his account to relate a story which it would please us all to hear. If you wish to enjoy my favor, start from the very beginning."

"I assure you, Lady, what you ask me to do is very painful to me and I would rather suffer one of my eyes to be plucked out than tell my story, were it not that I fear to incur your wrath. I will do what seems fitting to you, however much it may pain me. Since it is pleasing to you, now hear me. Lend me your heart and your ears. For even if heard, a word is lost if it is not understood in the heart. Some people hear but do not heed and yet they offer praise. They have merely the faculty of hearing because the heart does not understand at all. The word comes to the ears just as does the wind, but it does not stop or tarry. Rather, it leaves in a very short time if the heart is not awakened so that it is ready to seize it. For when it comes, the heart alone can grasp, absorb, and retain

3

it. The ears are the path and the channel by which the voice reaches the heart, and the heart then takes into one's being the voice which enters by way of the ear. Now, whoever wishes to attend must give me heart and ears, for I do not wish to speak about a dream or a fable or a lie. Many another has dealt thus with you, but I intend to relate to you exactly what I witnessed.

"It happened nearly seven years ago that, solitary as a fieldworker, I set out seeking adventure in full armor as befits a knight. I found a road on the right hand leading through a dense forest. The way was very wild, choked with thorns and thistles. I followed the path with considerable pain and difficulty nearly the whole day but continued riding until I issued from the Forest of Brocéliande. From the forest, I entered upon a plain and saw a wooden castle half a Welsh league beyond, so far but no more. I proceeded to that place at a rate faster than a walk and gazed on the palisade and the deep, broad moat surrounding it. On the bridge stood the man to whom the castle belonged, a moulted falcon on his wrist. I had no more than greeted him when he came to hold my stirrup and invited me to dismount. I complied, for I was sadly in need of lodgings. He remarked more than a hundred times altogether that the road by which I had come there was blessed. We then entered the courtyard, passing over the drawbridge and through the gate. Within the courtyard of the vavasour [untitled landholder], to whom may God accord such joy and honor as he showed to me that night, there hung a gong. I believe that it was not made of iron or wood or of anything other than copper. The vavasour sounded the gong three times with a hammer which hung nearby on a post. Those who were indoors heard the talking and the noise and came out of the hall and down into the courtyard. One of them took my horse, which the good vavasour had been holding.

"Then I saw approaching me a beautiful and noble maiden

4

and gave myself over to gazing upon her for she was tall, slender, and straight. She was skilful in disarming me; indeed, she performed this task properly and graciously, and then she attired me in a short cloak of peacock-blue and vari-colored material. All the people left us there and no one remained with us, which suited me, for I wished for nothing more than to look at her. She took me and sat me down in the most beautiful little meadow in the world enclosed all around by a low wall. I found her so well-mannered, so fair of speech, so properly schooled, and of such pleasing appearance and presence that it delighted me greatly to be there, and I had no wish to leave. But on that evening, the vavasour annoyed me a great deal by summoning me when it was the time to sup. Since I could not delay longer, I did his bidding at once. About the supper, I will speak briefly. It was altogether to my liking because the damsel was seated before me. After supper, the vavasour told me that he could not recall the time when he had had as guest a knight errant in search of adventure, although he had lodged many a warrior. And he said further that he would be rewarded if I were to return by way of his abode, if I could. I told him, 'Gladly, Sir.' For it would have been shameful to refuse him. Little would I be doing for my host if I were to deny him this request.

"I was very well lodged that night, and my horse was saddled as soon as one could see the daylight. On the previous night I had earnestly requested that this be done, and my desire had been acted upon. I commended my good host and his dear daughter to the Holy Spirit and begged permission to leave as soon as possible. I had scarcely set out from the castle when I saw in a clearing wild bulls at large fighting among themselves. They stirred up a great noise and were so wild and savage that I drew back out of timidity, to tell you the truth. For there is no beast as fierce or mad as a bull. I then saw, seated on a tree stump with a great bludgeon in his hand, a lout who resembled a Moor, huge and exceedingly hideous. He was so very ugly a creature that no words could describe him. I came closer to the wretch and saw that his head was greater than that of a nag or any other animal. His hair was in tufts and his naked forehead was more than two spans in breadth. He had great mossy ears like an elephant's, heavy eyebrows, a flat face, the eyes of a screech-owl, a nose like a cat's, a mouth shaped like a wolf's, the teeth of a boar, sharp and yellowed, and a black beard and twisted moustaches. His chin met his chest, and he had a long backbone, crooked and humped. He leaned on his club, and he was dressed in a strange mantle made neither of linen nor wool. Rather, he had fastened about his neck two hides of recently flayed bulls or oxen.

"When he saw me draw near, the churl jumped at once to his feet. I do not know whether he planned to strike me or what else he may have intended, but I prepared to defend myself. Then I saw that he stood very quietly and that he did not move. He had climbed up on a tree trunk and he was certainly seventeen feet tall. He stared at me and spoke no word any more than an animal. I decided that he lacked reason and therefore did not know how to talk. But nevertheless, I ventured to say: 'See here, tell me whether you are a creature of good or not?' And he replied to me, 'I am a man.' 'What kind of man are you?' 'Such as you see here. I have never been otherwise.' 'What are you doing here?' 'I am here to herd these animals of the forest.' 'Herd them? By Saint Peter of Rome, they do not obey any man. I do not believe that one can herd wild animals in field or in thicket or in any other place by any means unless they are tethered or enclosed by a fence.' 'Yet, I herd and tend these to keep them from leaving this place.' 'And how? Tell me the truth!' 'There is not one of them that dares stir when it sees me coming. For when I must capture one of them, I force it down by its two horns with my hands, which are tough and strong, in such a manner that the rest tremble with fear, and they all crowd around me as if to cry for mercy. No one, if placed in their midst, could trust himself to them except me, for forthwith he would be killed. Thus I am master of my beasts. But you on your part ought to tell me what sort of man you are and what you are looking for here.'

" 'I am, as you see, a knight who seeks what he is not able to find. I have searched a good while but have found nothing.' 'And what do you think you will find?' 'Adventures, which will put my knighthood and my endurance to the test. Now, I beg of you to advise me, if you can, where there may be an adventure or some marvelous thing.' 'In this you surely will have no luck,' he said, 'for I know nothing about adventures nor have I heard any spoken about. Yet, if you were to go to a spring nearby, you would not return without some difficulty, provided that you abide by the local custom. Hard by you will find a path which will lead you to it. Keep straight on it, if you would make good use of your steps, for there are many other paths and you would soon be led astray. Then you will see a spring which boils even though it is colder than marble. The most beautiful tree which Nature ever made casts its shade over it. The foliage remains on the tree all the time, for it is not lost in the winter. An iron basin hangs there by a chain long enough to reach to the spring. Near the spring you will find a stone (I do not know how to describe it for I have never seen another like it), and on the other side stands a chapel, small in size but very beautiful. If you will fill the basin with water and pour it over the stone, you will experience such a storm that no beast will remain in the forest. The roebucks, does, red deer, wild boars, and birds will all rush forth, and you will see such flashes of lightning, such wind, such crashing of trees, and such rain, and you will hear such thunder that, if you succeed in leaving without great injury and distress, you will be more fortunate than those knights who have been there before you.'

"I then left the lout who had shown me the trail. I believe that it was past tierce [about 9:00 A.M.] and it may have been near midday when I saw the tree and the chapel. In truth, I

7

well recognized that the tree was the most beautiful pine that ever grew on earth. I do not believe that it ever rained so hard that a single drop of water dampened the trunk. Rather, the rain would all run off the outer foliage. Near the tree I saw hanging a basin of the finest gold that was ever yet on sale at any market. With respect to the spring, you must understand that it bubbled like boiling water. The stone was an emerald, pierced much like a cask, and it had four rubies beneath more ruddy and sparkling than the sun when it rises in the east in the morning. I will not knowingly tell you a single untruth.

"I wished particularly to see the miracle of the storm and the tempest, of which I knew nothing as yet. But I would straightway have repented had I been able to do so when I sprinkled the perforated stone with water from the basin. I fear that I poured out too much water, for I saw the sky so rent apart that the lightning flashed in my eyes from more than fourteen directions, and the clouds shed mingled snow, rain, and hail. So severe and terrible was the storm that I thought I would be killed on a hundred occasions by the thunderbolts which struck all around me and by the trees which were torn to pieces. You must realize that I was utterly terrified until the tempest abated. But God comforted me, for the storm did not continue long, and then the winds diminished. They dare not blow if it is not pleasing to God.

"When I felt the clear, pure air, I was filled again with joy. For happiness, as I have observed, soon causes great distress to be forgotten. When the tempest had ceased, I saw so many birds clustered on the pine tree, if any will believe me, that there was no branch or bit of foliage that was not covered with them. The tree was then the more beautiful, and all the birds sang so that they accorded one with another, yet each of them sang a different tune. Never did I hear one of them sing the same song as another. I was delighted by their happiness, and I listened until they had finished all their service in a leisurely way. Never have I heard such great joy nor do

I think that any other man will hear it unless he goes there to listen to what pleased and charmed me so much that I was beside myself.

"I was in this state when I thought I heard a knight coming. Rather, I thought there were ten, so great was the noise and clatter aroused by the single knight who appeared. When I saw him coming on alone, I tightened my saddle girths and did not delay mounting my horse. With evil intent he rushed on more swiftly than a great bird, and he was as fierce as a lion in appearance. From as far off as he could make himself heard, he began to challenge me and shouted: 'Vassal! You have brought great shame and injury to me without just cause. You ought to have brought an accusation against me if there were a feud between us or pled your cause at least before you stirred up strife. But, Sir Vassal, as much as lies in my power, I will repay you for the damage you have clearly done. About me is the evidence of my forest, which has been devastated. A man who is injured ought to protest. I complain, as I have good reason to do, that you have driven me from my house by thunderbolts and rain. You have done a thing which injures me, and may he who thinks it good be accursed. On my own forest and my castle you have leveled such an attack that the aid of men or of arms or of fortifications would have been of no avail. Even if he had been in a castle of hard stone or of wood, a man would not have been safe. Understand plainly that henceforth you will have no peace or truce with me!'

"With this word, we came together. We held our shields on our arms, and each of us protected himself therewith. The knight had a good horse and a stout lance and, without doubt, was taller by a full head than I. Thus, I was altogether in ill luck, for I was smaller than he, and his horse was the stronger. (You must realize that I intend to tell the whole truth in order to explain how my humiliation came about.) I gave him as heavy a blow as I could strike with all my heart, hitting the top of his shield and exerting all my strength so that my

9

lance flew to bits. His lance remained whole, however, for it was not light in weight. Rather, in my opinion, it was heavier than the lance of any other knight, and I never saw one so large. The knight in his turn struck me so violently that he thrust me over my horse's rump flat on the ground, where he left me stretched out and exhausted. He did not so much as glance back at me but, taking my horse and leaving, he returned to the roadway. Completely at a loss, I stayed there confused and bewildered. Seating myself near the spring, I rested for a little while. I dared not pursue the knight because I feared that I would commit some foolish act. And even if I dared follow, I did not know what had become of him.

"At last, I recalled that I had made an agreement with my host to return to him. This thought seemed pleasant to me and I acted on it. But first I laid aside all my arms in order to travel light and thus shamefully returned. When I arrived that night at the castle, I found my host just the same, just as amiable and courteous as I had found him before. I perceived nothing at all in the demeanor of the daughter or the vavasour to suggest that they received me less willingly, nor did they accord me less respect than they had done the previous night. They all showed me great worship in that household out of their graciousness, and they stated that never before had anyone escaped from that place I had visited without being killed or kept prisoner, so far as they knew or had heard. Thus I departed and thus I returned, and on my return I accounted myself a fool. And, like a fool, I have told you what I never wanted to reveal."

*　　*　　*

"By my head!" said my Lord Ywain, "You are my cousin and we ought to love each other. Yet, I must pronounce you stupid because you have concealed this from me so long. If I have called you stupid, I beg that it not distress you. For if I can, and if I am permitted to do so, I shall set out to avenge your humiliation." "It is indeed clear that it is after dinner-

10

time," said Kay, who did not know how to keep quiet. "There are more words in a pot of wine than in a measure of beer. They say that a drunken cat becomes gay. After dinner, without stirring forth, everybody is ready to slay Sultan Noradin and you are setting out to take vengeance on King Forré [perform great exploits and make empty boasts]. Are your saddle-pads stuffed and your iron greaves polished and your banners displayed? Now then, in the name of God, my Lord Ywain, will you start tonight or tomorrow? Please to inform us, fair Sir, when you will go off to this ordeal for we would like to accompany you. There is no provost or sheriff who would not gladly escort you. And, however it may be, I beg that you do not go without bidding us goodbye. But, if you have a bad dream tonight, stay at home!"

"The Devil! Are you mad, my Lord Kay?" said the Queen. "Does your tongue never cease? May shame befall the tongue which is so bitter. Indeed, your tongue hates you, for it says all the worst things it knows to everyone, whoever he may be. May the tongue be accursed which never tires of speaking foully. Your tongue behaves in such a way as to make you detested everywhere. It could do you no greater dishonor. You may be sure of this: I would attaint it of treason, if it were mine. A man who cannot profit by chastisement ought to be bound in front of the choir-screen in church like a lunatic."

"Truly, my Lady," said my Lord Ywain, "his taunts do not upset me. My Lord Kay is so resourceful, wise, and worthy in every court that he would never be taciturn or deaf. He knows well how to reply to baseness with reason and courtesy, and he never did otherwise. Now, you know well if I lie. But I have no wish to quarrel or to resume our foolish behavior. That man does not always win the skirmish who strikes the first blow, but rather the one who succeeds in avenging himself. It is better that one fight a stranger than that he contend against a comrade. I have no wish to emulate the watchdog that bristles and shows his teeth whenever another dog snarls at him."

11

While they were speaking thus, the King came out of the bower where until this moment he had remained a long time asleep. The barons, when they saw him, all sprang to their feet, but he caused them all to sit down again. As he seated himself beside the Queen, she recounted word for word all of Calogrenant's story, for she knew well how to tell a tale properly. The King listened to her eagerly, then he swore three strong oaths—on the soul of Utherpendragon, his father, and on the souls of his son and his mother—that he would set out before two weeks should have passed to see the spring, the tempest, and the marvels. If he could arrive by the Vigil of the Feast of my Lord Saint John the Baptist, he would take his night's rest there. And he announced that all who wished might accompany him. The entire court approved highly of the plan which the King described, and the barons and young knights hoped very much to go with him.

But, whoever else might be merry and joyous, my Lord Ywain was disappointed because he had hoped to go by himself. He was therefore chagrined and vexed with the King for arranging to undertake the journey. It grieved him for this reason: he knew well that my Lord Kay without doubt would venture the combat. If he so desired, it would not be refused him. Again, my Lord Gawain might petition for it first, perhaps. If either of these two pressed his claim, the favor would not be denied him. But he did not wait because he had no desire for their company. Therefore, he would set out alone, if he could manage it, whether the result would be to his profit or loss. And, whoever remained at home, he at least expected to be in Brocéliande on the third day and attempt, if he could, to find the narrow, heavily-wooded path, for which he was most eager, and the meadow, the strong castle, the pleasure and charm of the courteous damsel so accomplished and beautiful, and the gracious man, who, along with his daughter, exerted himself to provide dignified hospitality and was so generous and of such great worth. Then would he see the bulls in the clearing and the great lout

12

who herded them. He was impatient to see a creature who was loathsome, huge, hideous, misshapen, and as swarthy as a blacksmith. Then would he see, if he could, the stone, the spring, the basin, and the birds on the pine tree, and he would cause it to rain and blow. Yet he would not boast about it until he should have reaped either great shame or great worship. Then the affair could be made known.

My Lord Ywain departed from the court. He encountered no man and went alone to his lodgings. There he found all his household and gave orders for his horse to be saddled and for one of his squires from whom he concealed nothing to come to him. "Listen!" he said. "Come outside after me and bring my arms. I will leave by that gate on my palfrey at a walk. Do not delay, for it is necessary that I travel a great distance. See that my war horse is well shod and lead him quietly after me. Afterwards, you will lead my palfrey back. But, heed carefully, I command you. If anyone should question you about me, give him no news. Otherwise, you may not count on me hereafter whether or not you now have any confidence in me." "Sir," said he, "all will be well. No one will know about it from me. Go forth and I will follow."

My Lord Ywain now mounted. If he could, he wished to avenge his cousin's defeat before his return. The squire ran for arms and for his war horse and mounted. He did not delay, for the horse lacked neither shoes nor nails. He followed his lord's trail until he saw him on foot for he had waited a little distance from the road in a secluded spot. The squire brought him his harness and equipment and accoutered him. My Lord Ywain did not tarry at all after he had been armed but traveled a considerable distance each day over mountains, through valleys and great, broad forests, and by strange, wild places. He crossed many treacherous straits and survived many a peril and many a danger until he came to the very narrow path full of thorns and dark shadows. There he felt reassured because he could not now go astray. Whatever the cost, he would not leave off until he saw the pine tree

13

which shaded the spring, and the stone, and the storm with its hail, rain, thunder, and lightning. He found that night, as you may know, such a host as he had hoped for, and he received a greater measure of good will and respect at the hands of the vavasour than had been told to him. And in the damsel he found one hundred times the wit and beauty that Calogrenant had promised. But one cannot express the full value of a fine lady or a worthy man. Never can all features of one who has devoted himself to virtue be completely described or told, nor tongue set forth the honorable deeds of such a person.

My Lord Ywain had good lodgings that night and that pleased him much. The next day he proceeded to the clearing and saw the bulls and the country lout who pointed out the path to him. But he crossed himself more than a hundred times at the sight of that marvelous creature before him and wondered how Nature could have made one so ugly and loathsome. Then he came upon the spring and everything else he had hoped to see. Without pausing and without sitting down, he poured a very full basin of water directly on the stone. Thereupon it stormed and rained and blew a gale, as it was expected to do. And when God restored fine weather, the birds appeared in the pine tree and were very joyous above the perilous spring. But, before their jubilation had stopped, there came a knight more burning with wrath than a glowing ember and with as much clatter as is made by chasing a stag in rut. And at once the two rushed at each other and engaged in battle, showing that they hated each other to the death. They both bore heavy, strong lances with which they delivered violent blows that shattered the shields about their necks and tore each other's hauberk to bits. Their lances splintered and shattered and the fragments flew high in the air. Then they set on each other with swords so that in the clash of their weapons they cut the shield straps and split the shields with the result that the shreds hung down above and below and they no longer served to protect them.

14

They slashed at each other so much with their gleaming swords that they struck sides, arms, and hips without hindrance. Savagely they tested each other, yet they did not move from their positions any more than two stone blocks. Never were two knights so eager to bring about each other's death. They did not wish to waste blows but delivered them as best they could. Their helms became dented and bent and links of mail flew from their hauberks so that they drew a good deal of blood. Their hauberks grew so hot from their bodies that they were scarcely of more protection than a cowl. As they thrust at each other's face, it is a wonder that such a bitter and prolonged combat could continue. But both were of such great courage that neither would yield a foot of ground to the other until he had given him his death wound. Yet, they were most careful not to injure or wound each other's horse. They did not wish nor would they condescend to do such a thing. At all times they kept their saddles, never setting foot to ground, and therefore the duel was the more admirable. At length, my Lord Ywain battered to pieces his adversary's helm. He was made deaf and faint by this blow, for he had never before received one so pitiless. He had split his skull under his head piece down to the brain so that the mail links of his bright hauberk were stained with blood and brains, and from this cause he felt such intense agony that his courage failed him somewhat.

Then he fled, and he was not wrong in so doing, for he believed that he had suffered a mortal wound and that further opposition would avail nothing. As soon as he had collected his wits, he fled at once toward his town at a gallop. The drawbridge was lowered for him and the gates were opened wide. My Lord Ywain spurred impetuously after him as fast as he could. Just as a gerfalcon swoops after a crane appearing afar off and approaches so closely that he thinks he will seize it, and yet fails to strike, so the knight took flight and the other pursued him so hard that he could almost touch him. Yet he did not quite reach him even though he was close enough to hear him moan from the pain. All this time, the one gave himself up to flight and the other strove to catch him. Ywain feared his efforts would be in vain if he did not capture him dead or alive. He recalled the insults which my Lord Kay had hurled at him; nor was he quit of the promise he had given his cousin, for he would not by any means be believed unless he could bring back reliable evidence. The knight led him at a gallop to the gates of the town and they both entered. They found no man or woman in the streets through which they passed, and both came at great speed to the gates of the palace.

The gate was very high and broad, but it had so narrow an entrance that two men or two horses could not enter, nor could both ride abreast through the passage without jostling or great difficulty. It was constructed just like a trap with a hidden blade above, which has been set for an ill-intentioned rat. Such a blade will drop, strike, and impale, for it is at once released so that it falls when anything trips the spring however gently. In like manner, there were two devices underneath the gate which held up on high an iron portcullis, ground sharp and cutting. If anyone stepped on the trigger, the portcullis fell from above and whoever was below would be transfixed and completely mangled. The passageway exactly in the middle of the gate was as narrow as a beaten path. Straight through this defile rushed the knight very skilfully. My Lord Ywain hurtled on madly at full speed, and he approached the other so closely that he held on to his saddle. This circumstance was very fortunate for him for he had stretched his body forward. He would have been cut through had this not been the case, for his horse stepped on the beam which released the iron portcullis. Just like a devil from hell, the gate slid down, struck the saddle and the horse behind slicing through them completely. Yet, thanks be to God, it did not touch Ywain, except that when it grazed him along his back it sheared off his spurs flush with his heels. Ywain fell down astounded, but the other, who was mortally wounded, escaped from him in this manner: there was another port-cullis farther on like the one behind him. The knight, as he fled, passed through the gate, and the second portcullis fell after him.

Thus was my Lord Ywain imprisoned. Greatly alarmed and distressed, he remained behind in the sealed room, the roof of which was set with gilded nails, and the walls were painted in a splendid fashion in rich colors. But he was not so much troubled about anything as he was about not knowing where the knight had gone. While he was anxiously pacing up and down, he heard a narrow door open, and a damsel entered alone. She was very attractive and handsome. She closed the door after her, and when she found my Lord Ywain, she was at first astonished. "Indeed, Sir Knight," said she, "I fear you come at an evil time. For my lord is mortally wounded, and I know well that you have slain him. My lady is in frenzied mourning and her people about her are weeping so that they nearly kill themselves for grief. But the sorrow among them is so great that they cannot yet act. Still, if they wish to kill or seize you, they cannot fail to do so whenever they choose." And my Lord Ywain replied, "If it please God, they will not kill me. I will not be taken by them." "No," she said, "for I will do all for you that is in my power. That man is not at all valiant who is too fearful. I believe you to be a brave man who is not utterly dismayed. Understand clearly that, if I may, I will render you service and honor such as you would do for me. Once my lady sent me to the court of the King on an errand. I suppose that I was not so prudent, or courteous, or well-mannered as a maiden ought to be, for there was not a knight who condescended to speak a single word to me except for you, who stand here. Out of your great compassion, you used me honorably and were of service to me. Because of the treatment which you accorded me, I offer you this help. I know your name very well and know who you are: you are the son of King Urien and are called Sir Ywain. Now you may be reassured and at your

17

ease, for you will never be captured or injured if you are willing to trust me. Take my little ring, and, if you please, give it back to me when I shall have rescued you."

She then gave him the little ring, explaining that it had the same effect as the bark of a tree which covers the wood so that one cannot see it at all. It was necessary that one wear the ring with the stone inside the fist. Whoever had the ring on his finger need not be wary of anything, for no man could see him however wide his eyes were open any more than he could see the wood covered by the bark growing over it. This was pleasing to my Lord Ywain. When she had told him this, she made him sit down on a bed covered with a counterpane so rich that even the Duke of Austria did not have its equal. Then she said that, if he wished, she would bring him food, and he replied that it would be welcome. The damsel then ran swiftly to her bower and returned very soon bringing a capon, a roast, a cake, a table cloth, and wine of good vintage in a full pot covered with a white goblet. These things she offered him to eat, and he, who was in need, ate and drank very gladly.

By the time he had eaten and drunk, the knights were on the move searching for him within. They wished to avenge their lord, who had been placed on his bier. Then she said to him: "Friend, do you hear all those who are looking for you? They are making a great deal of noise and commotion. But do not move on account of the noise whoever may come or go. You will not be discovered if you do not stir from this bed. You will see this room full of the most hostile and ill-intentioned men who will expect to find you here. I suspect that they will bring the corpse here before they place it in the grave, and they will begin searching for you under benches and beds. It will be a sport and a delight to one who is without fear to see such blind men. For they will all be so sightless, so frustrated, and so deluded that they will be transported with rage. I cannot talk any more with you now because I dare not remain longer. But I would offer thanks to God for

18

having given me the occasion and the opportunity of doing something which is pleasing to you and for which I had a very great desire."

When she had gone her way, all the people assembled from both sides of the gate carrying cudgels and swords. There was a very great multitude and a dense crowd of desperate and angry people. They saw in front of the portcullis the half of the horse which had been sliced in two parts, and they were very certain that when they should open the gates they would find inside the man they sought to kill. They then caused the portcullis, by which many men had been killed, to be drawn up. But, since there was no trap or snare set for their entrance, they came through abreast. On the inside, over the threshold, they found the other half of the slain horse. Yet, not an eye among them could discern my Lord Ywain, whom they would have slain most gladly. He saw them enraged, maddened, and infuriated. They said: "How can this be? There is no door or window through which anything could pass unless it were a bird which flies or a squirrel or a marmot or some animal just as small or smaller. For the windows are fastened and the portcullis closed through which my lord escaped. Dead or alive, the body is inside. Outside, nothing at all remains, and within we see more than half of the saddle, yet we see no trace of him except for the severed spurs which fell from his feet. Now, let us search in all the corners and leave off this vain chatter! It appears that he is still inside, or we are bespelled, or else demons have snatched him away from us!"

Heated with wrath, they all sought for him in the chamber, beating on the walls, the beds, and the benches. But the bed on which he lay was passed over and spared their blows and he was neither struck nor touched. There was much floundering about, and they set up a great turmoil with their clubs just as does a blind man who stumblingly goes tapping about searching for something. As they continued ransacking under the beds and stools, there entered one of the most beautiful ladies that mortal man ever saw. Notice or heed was never taken of so fair a Christian lady, but she was so frenzied by grief that she was near to killing herself. From time to time she cried out in a loud voice and then fell down in a faint. And when she was raised up, she began, like a distracted woman, to rend herself and tear her hair. She clawed her hair and ripped her clothing and swooned at every step. Nothing could quiet her when she saw her lord borne in before her dead on his bier. She believed that she could never again be happy and for that reason she wept very loudly. The holy water, the cross, and the candles were first carried in by nuns from a convent, then came the gospel-books, the censer, and the clerics who were charged with administering the solemn absolution needful for the miserable soul.

Sir Ywain heard the lamenting and the grief which cannot be described because no one would be able to depict it nor was such ever written in a book. The cortège passed by, but a great tumult arose around the bier in the center of the room, for the warm blood, clear and red, flowed from the wounds of the dead man. This was certain proof that, without fail, the one who had waged the fight and had slain and conquered him was still inside. Thereupon they searched and pried everywhere and hunted and stirred about so much that they were all bathed in sweat from their distress and turmoil, because of the red blood which trickled down before them. Sir Ywain was struck and jostled a good deal where he lay, but he in no wise moved for all that. And the people grew more and more disturbed by the wounds which had opened up. They wondered why they bled but they did not know where to lay the blame. Each and every one spoke: "Among us is the one who killed him, yet we do not see him at all. This is a mysterious and devilish thing."

Thereupon, the lady exhibited such grief that she seemed beside herself and cried out as if demented: "Oh God! Will no one then find the homicide, the traitor, who killed my good lord? Good? Truly he was the best of good men. True God, the injustice will be yours if you permit him to escape in this way. I can blame none other than you because you have stolen him away from my sight. Never was seen such violence or such grievous wrong as you do me, for you do not allow me to see that one who is so near at hand. Indeed, I may say that, since I do not see him, some phantom or demon has come between us here so that I am wholly bewitched. Or is he a coward who fears me? Fainthearted is he to be in such terror of me. Refusal to reveal himself before me comes from abject timidity. Ah, phantom, cowardly thing! Why are you so fearful of me when you were so valiant in the presence of my lord? Vain thing, weak thing! Why do I not now have you in my power? Why can I not now seize you? How could it happen that you killed my lord unless you did it by treachery? Surely my lord would never have been vanquished by you had he caught sight of you. There was not his equal in the whole world, nor does God or man know of another, nor is there likely ever again to be one. Certainly, if you were a mortal man you would not have dared fight my lord, for no one was capable of withstanding him."

Thus the lady reasoned with herself; thus within herself she complained, thus she tormented and confounded herself. And the people with her fell again into such great lamentation that they could not grieve more. They carried off the body to inter it, and then they searched and bestirred themselves so violently that they were wholly exhausted by their pursuit. They gave it up because of their fatigue when they were unable to find anyone who had done anything of a suspicious nature. The nuns and the priest, having already finished the office of the dead and returned to the church, then approached the place of burial. The damsel in her bower paid no attention to all this, but she recalled my Lord Ywain and came to him very soon, saying: "Fair Sir, these people have been after you in very large numbers. They have stormed about in here a great deal and have rummaged through all these hiding places more thoroughly than a hound sets out to flush a par-

tridge or quail. No doubt you were in a great state of fright."
"By my faith," said he, "you speak the truth! I never thought
I should experience such great terror. Yet, if it could be arranged, I should like very much to watch the funeral procession and the body through some chink or window." But, he
had no real concern either with the corpse or the procession.
In fact, he would just as soon see them all burned up even
though it were to cost him a thousand marks. A thousand?
In truth, on my faith, three thousand! Rather, he said this
because it was the mistress of the castle whom he hoped to
see.

The damsel placed him at a little window and thus repaid
him as best she could for the courtesy he had shown her.
Through this window my Lord Ywain watched the beautiful
lady. The lady spoke: "Fair Lord, may God truly have mercy
on your soul. Never, to my knowledge, was there a knight in
saddle who was so worthy in any way as you. Nor was there
ever a knight who possessed your degree of honor or your
courtesy, fair dear one. Generosity was your friend and valor
your companion. May your soul be in the company of the
saints, fair, sweet knight." Thereupon she struck and clutched
at whatever her hands could reach. With great difficulty my
Lord Ywain restrained himself from running out to hold her
hands, whatever might happen. But the damsel implored,
counseled, commanded, and scolded him, although in the
manner of a courteous person of good breeding, that he
beware of doing anything foolish, and said: "You are very
well off here. Do not move for any cause until this outburst
of grief is moderated and these people have taken their leave,
for they will depart soon. If you will abide by my advice, as
I will give it to you, you will reap great benefit. Be quiet and
remain seated while watching the people who pass along their
way both inside and out. Not one of them will see you, and
thus you will hold a very great advantage. But beware of
speaking out imprudently, for whoever acts rashly and is
carried away and exerts himself to perform some foolish deed

whenever he has the chance and the occasion, that one I consider more stupid than wise. If you are contemplating something impulsive, see to it that you do not carry it out. The wise man hides his silly thoughts and tries, if he can, to accomplish something good instead. Watch out, then, like a prudent man, and do not put your head in jeopardy, for those people out there would not accept any ransom for it. Have a care for yourself and bear my advice in mind. Now, be at ease, for I am going and may not remain here longer. Quite possibly, I might stay here so long that they would suspect me, especially if they were not to see me in the crowd of people, and then I would be severely punished."

She then left and Ywain stayed behind, not knowing how to act. With respect to the corpse which he saw the people bury, it distressed him that he did not have some memento that would give evidence on his behalf of his having vanquished and slain his foe and which he could exhibit openly. If he were to have no testimony or proof, he would be shamed through and through. For Kay was so ill-natured and perverse, so full of taunts and anger, that he would never be safe from him. He would go about constantly insulting him and hurling jests and taunts just as he had done the other day. These indignities continued to fester anew in his heart. Yet, with sugar and honey-comb the new Love was now taming him. Love had conducted a raid on his land and had succeeded completely in taking her quarry. His enemy had led away his heart, for he loved that one who most detested him. Although she did not realize it, the lady had fully vindicated her lord's death. She had received a greater requital than she could ever have achieved had Love not avenged her by assailing him so sweetly, piercing his heart through his eyes. This wound would last longer than any wound made by lance or sword. A sword cut heals and becomes whole very soon when a physician attends to it, but the wound made by Love becomes the worse the nearer it is to its physician. My Lord Ywain had received a hurt which would never be healed, for Love had devoted herself wholly to him. She then went about searching those places which she formerly haunted in order to remove from them every particle of herself. She desired no lodgings nor host other than this new one. She acted wisely in giving up poor lodgings because she ought to be entirely his. She did not wish that there be anything of herself elsewhere, and she searched all those inferior hostelries. It is a pity that Love is such an individual and that she shows herself so base as to select the most unsuitable dwellings and to remain there just as readily as in the best. But now she was welcome where she would be held in esteem and where she ought indeed to stay. Love ought to conduct herself thus because she is a high-born creature and it is a marvel how she would dare to descend so shamefully into vile places. She resembles one who sprinkles her fragrant balm on ashes and dust, who hates honor and loves shame, mingles sugar with gall, and stirs together soot and honey. But, on this occasion, she did not do this; rather, she took up lodgings in a noble place for which no one could reproach her.

When the dead man had been buried, all the people left. No cleric, knight, retainer, or lady remained there except that one who did not conceal her grief. She stayed there all alone, grasping herself by the throat, twisting her fingers, and beating her hands together as she read psalms from a psalter illuminated with letters of gold. Meanwhile, my Lord Ywain still watched her from the window, and the more he paid heed to her the more he loved her and was charmed by her. He wished that she would cease to weep and read and that it were possible for him to speak to her. Love, who had seized him at the window, put him into this state. But, he despaired of attaining his desire and could not believe that his hopes could ever be fulfilled. He said: "I consider myself a fool to desire something I cannot have. I wounded her lord to the death. Do I think that I can make my peace with her? By my faith! I would not be wise to think it possible, for she abhors me now more than anything, and she is right in so doing. In saying this, I have spoken truly: still, a woman has more than a thousand hearts. The frame of mind she is in at present, I believe, will change soon. Indeed, she will doubtless alter it, and I would be foolish to despair. May God grant that it soon change! I must be in her power all my days, for Love decrees it.

"Whoever does not accept Love gladly when she draws near him commits an abomination and an act of treason. And I say (whoever is so minded let him heed this), that such a person does not deserve a good life or happiness. Because I do not wish to lose out, I would love my enemy. Unless I should wish to frustrate Love, I may not hate her. That one whom Love chooses, it is up to me to love. And should she consider me her friend? Yes, by all means, because I am in love with her. And yet I acknowledge her my enemy, she who hates me, and she is not wrong in so doing, because I have slain the one she loved. And am I, then, her enemy? No indeed, but rather her friend, for never before have I desired so much to love. I pine for her beautiful hair which shines so that it surpasses fine gold. It kindles and inflames me with passion when I see her tear at it and pull it out. Never could the tears which stream from her eyes be dried. All this makes me unhappy. Even though they are brimming with tears, of which there is no end or conclusion, there were never such exquisite eyes. The fact that she weeps pains me, and I have never suffered such anguish as at the sight of her face, which she mutilates even though it has not deserved such treatment. I never saw a face so admirably shaped or so fresh or possessed of such a complexion. And it distresses me a great deal when I see her clutch her throat. Indeed, she cannot refrain from doing her worst. There is no crystal or mirror which is so clear and radiant. O, God! Why does she indulge in such great folly, and why does she not torture herself less? Why does she wring her beautiful hands and beat and claw her breast? Would she not be wondrously fine to gaze upon if she were calm, she who is now so handsome even though

25

distraught? Yes, certainly. I can swear to that. Never again could Nature so overstep the mark with respect to beauty. She far surpassed herself. Could she ever, perchance, make such another? How could this have come about in the first place? Where did such great beauty come from? Indeed, God created her with his bare hand in order to make Nature stare. She would have to devote all her time to it if she hoped to make one like her, and even then she could not accomplish it. Even God, should he wish to exert himself, could not succeed, I think, in making another one whatever the effort he might put forth."

Thus my Lord Ywain mused on that one who was tormenting herself with grief. I do not believe that any man in captivity, in danger of losing his head like my Lord Ywain, would ever love so madly the very person whose favors he could never seek. Nor could it be that there was someone who would intercede for him. He watched at the window until the lady departed and both portcullises were lowered. Any other man, who preferred deliverance to remaining behind, would have been disturbed. But to Ywain, it was all one whether the gates were closed or open. Indeed, he would not have gone away if they had been left open, not even had the lady given him permission to go and pardoned him voluntarily for the death of her lord so that he could depart in safety. But Love and Shame detained him, assailing him from two sides. He would be disgraced if he went away now because no one would believe that he had acquitted himself so well. On the other hand, he felt so strong a desire to look at least upon the beautiful lady, even if only this, that he was not concerned about his imprisonment. He would have died sooner than go away. Then the damsel returned, wishing to be in his company and to entertain and amuse him, bringing whatever he asked for. But she found him pensive and languid. She said: "My Lord Ywain, how have you spent this day?" "Very pleasantly," said he. "Pleasantly? Indeed! Are you speaking the truth? How is this? Unless one hopes or longs for death, how can he

26

have a pleasant time when he sees men who seek to kill him?"
"Truly, my sweet friend," said he, "I should not at all like to
die, and yet what I saw pleases me now and will always please
me." "Now, let us leave off talking of that," she said, "for I
can understand what this speech tends toward. I am not so
simple or foolish as not to comprehend such talk. But now,
follow me. For I shall take immediate steps to free you from
prison. In fact, I shall bring you to safety, if it please you,
either tonight or tomorrow. Now, come along. I will guide
you." But he replied: "You may be certain that I will not
this week run away like a thief. I would gain more honor by
leaving while all the people are gathered out there in the
streets." With this word, he went with her into a small room.
The damsel, who was clever and anxious to be of service to
him, provided whatever he needed. Then, when the occasion
arose, she recalled what he had told her—namely, that he
had been charmed a great deal by what he saw while those
who intended to kill him were searching the room for him.

The damsel was in such favor with her mistress that she
did not fear to tell her anything, whatever it might amount to,
for she was her adviser and her confidential attendant. Why,
then, should she be afraid to console her lady and remind
her of her dignity? At the first opportunity she told her
privately: "My Lady, it is a great marvel to me to see you
conduct yourself so foolishly. Do you think you can recover
your lord by mourning?" "By no means," said she, "but if I
had my wish, I would die of sorrow." "Why?" "In order to go
after him." "After him? May God forbid, and may he provide
you with as good a lord as possible." "You never spoke such
a lie, for he could not provide one so good." "A better one
would he give you if you would accept him, and I will prove
it." "Go away! Be quiet! I would never find such a man!"
"But you will, my Lady, if it please you. Now tell me, if it
is not too painful, who will protect your domain when King
Arthur comes, for he intends to arrive at the stone and the
spring next week? You have had word by the Savage Damsel,

27

who brought letters to you. Ah! What good service those letters did. You ought to give consideration to the defense of your spring, and yet you do not cease weeping. You must not delay, my dear Lady, if it please you. For certainly, as you well know, all the knights you have are not worth so much as a single chambermaid. Not even the one who considers himself the best will take up shield or lance. Of cowardly men you have many; in fact, not one is so courageous as to dare mount a horse. And the King is coming with so great a force that he will overcome everything without opposition."

The lady recognized this fully and considered that she had received good advice. But she had a foolish quality which other women also have; indeed, nearly all possess it even though they do not own their folly—namely, that they refuse the very thing they desire. "Go away!" said she. "Say no more. If I hear you mention this matter again, you would be ill-advised not to take flight. You talk so much that you weary me." "Very well, my Lady," said she. "It is indeed apparent that you are a woman, for a woman always becomes angry whenever she hears someone offer advice."

Then she departed. The lady reflected that she had been very much at fault. She particularly wanted to know how the damsel could have proved that a better knight than her lord was to be found. She would have listened very gladly, yet she had silenced her. She waited in this desire until her return. Then it was apparent that her command was not respected, for the damsel burst out at once: "Ah, my Lady. Is it now fitting that you kill yourself with grief? O, pray restrain yourself. Stop, if only out of shame. It does not beseem so high-born a lady to continue mourning so long. Keep in mind your rank and your great gentility. Do you think that all knightly prowess is dead along with your lord? A hundred as good as or better than he remain in the world." "If you do not lie, may God confound me! Name to me a single one who has the reputation of so valiant a man as my lord during his life." "You would bear me ill will and become angry and threaten me." "No, I will not, I assure you." "Then, it would be for your own good and it will turn out well for you if it would please you, and God grant that it does please you. I see no reason why I should be silent, for no one hears or attends us. You will consider me presumptuous, but I shall indeed say how it seems to me: When two knights in arms meet in combat, which one of them do you consider the better when one vanquishes the other? As for me, I should award the prize to the victor. What would you do?" "It seems to me that you want to catch me in my words." "On my faith! You should indeed listen, for I am keeping strictly to the truth. I shall prove to you that of necessity the one who defeated your lord is better than he was. He overpowered and pursued him vigorously right up to this point and besieged him in his own house." "Now have I heard," said she, "the greatest absurdity ever uttered! Go, you creature full of the evil spirit! Go, you mad and malicious hussy! Never speak such nonsense and never come into my presence again or say a single word on his behalf!" "Certainly, my Lady, I very well knew that I would not have your good will, and I told you that well in advance. But you made an agreement with me to the effect that you would not be antagonistic or angry with me for it. You have kept the bargain very poorly, but now you have spoken your mind and I suffer from breaking my prudent silence."

At that, she returned to her bower where she was maintaining Sir Ywain in great comfort. But nothing could please him when he learned that he could not see his lady, and he did not heed her or listen to a word of the account that the damsel rendered him. On her part, the lady all that night was at war with herself, for she felt great anxiety over the defense of her spring. She began to regret her conduct toward her whom she had reproached, insulted, and scorned. She was entirely certain in her mind that the damsel would not speak to her about him either for payment or for reward, or because she was fond of him. She knew that the damsel loved her more than she did him, and that she would not offer advice which would tend to shame or distress. She was too loyal a friend for that. Behold, how the lady changed toward her whom she had abused. She did not think that she could possibly love her again with all her heart. And that man, whom she had repulsed, she pardoned in justice and by force of argument very magnanimously, for he had done her no wrong. She then expressed her feelings just as if he had come there before her and began to argue in this wise: "Come," she said, "can you deny that through you my lord was slain?" "I cannot contradict that," he replied, "I fully acknowledge it." "Tell me, then, why? Did you do this out of malice toward me or out of hatred or scorn?" "May I have no respite from death if I did it out of malice toward you." "In that event, you have committed no offense toward me nor did you do him any wrong. For, if he could, he would have slain you. I think, then, that, to the best of my ability, I have judged well and equitably." In this way she found justice, plausibility, and reason in the situation, so that she felt no right to hate him. She argued in this manner, as she wished to do, and kindled a spark within herself so that she was like tinder smoking from the flame that has been set to it until someone blows up the fire and fans it. If the damsel were to appear now she would win the argument about which she had been so importunate and for which she had been much abused.

Indeed, she returned in the morning and resumed the argument at the point at which she had left off. Now the lady bowed her head, for she knew she had been wrong to insult her. She hoped now to make amends and to ask about the name, the rank, and the family of the knight. Like a wise woman, she humbled herself, saying: "I wish to ask your pardon for the wrath and pride with which I spoke to you, like a fool. I will abide by your counsel. Now, if you know, tell me about the knight on whose behalf you argued at such length. What sort of man is he and of what family? If he is

such that he is suitable for me, and if it should not fail to come about because of his attitude, I promise you that I will make him lord of my realm and of me. But it is necessary that he so conduct himself that no one can reproach me and say: 'This is she who took as husband the slayer of her lord.' "
"In the name of God, my Lady, thus it will be. You would have the noblest, the worthiest, and the most handsome lord to come from Abel's line." "What is his name?" "My Lord Ywain." "By my faith, this one is no churl. Rather, he is most noble, as I well know, if he is the son of King Urien." "By my faith, my Lady, you speak the truth." "When may we have him here?" "Within five days." "He would delay too long. I want him to come sooner than that. Let him be here tonight or tomorrow at the latest!" "My Lady, I do not think that any bird could fly so far in one day. But I shall send out one of my servants who can travel very fast, and he will reach King Arthur's court, I believe, at least by tomorrow in the evening, for Ywain will not be found nearer than that." "That period of time is still too great. The days are long. But tell him to be back tomorrow evening and command him to proceed more swiftly than he is accustomed. For, if he chooses to exert himself, he can make a two days' journey in one day. Also, the moon will be shining tonight and he may make the night into day. Upon his arrival, I will bestow on him whatever he wishes me to give him."

"Leave the details to me. You will have him in your hands by the third day from now, at the latest. Meanwhile, summon your people and take counsel with them about the King who will soon be here. In order to maintain the custom of defending your spring, it is fitting that you have good advice. There will not be one man among them so bold as to boast that he will go there. Then could you very properly announce that it is essential that you marry again. A certain very famous knight has asked for your hand, yet you dare not accept him unless they all advise you to do so. And I guarantee this, for I know them for cowards who would readily impose on another the burden that is too heavy for them: that they will all come to heel and render thanks to you because they would thereby be relieved of a great responsibility. For, whoever is afraid of his own shadow gladly shuns, if he can, any encounter with lance or throwing spear, for to a coward that appears to be a hard, dangerous sport." The lady replied; "By my faith! I wish it to be thus and I agree to it, for I had planned it just as you have described. Therefore, we will set about in this manner. But why are you dallying here? Go! Do not postpone doing anything that will help him! I shall remain with my people." Thus the conversation came to an end.

The damsel pretended to send out someone to seek my Lord Ywain in his own country, but on each day she caused him to be bathed, washed, and massaged. Moreover, she provided him with a robe of fine red material lined with fur with the chalk still on it. Nothing was lacking in his accoutrements that she did not supply: a clasp of gold to fasten at the neck ornamented with precious stones, which make people look very elegant and handsome, and a belt and purse made of splendid fabric. She dressed him completely and then informed her lady that her messenger had returned, having performed his mission like a competent man. "What?" said she. "When will my Lord Ywain come?" "He is here now." "Is he here? Then let him come privately and secretly while no one is with me. See to it that no more come in for I should greatly resent a fourth person." The damsel took her leave and returned to her guest. But she did not show in her face the happiness that possessed her heart. Rather, she said that her lady knew that she had been keeping him there and she said further: "Sir Ywain, indeed concealment is worth nothing now! The news about you has spread so far that my lady is aware of it, and she reproaches me and feels great anger and censures me heavily. But she has assured me that I may take you before her without danger or harm. She will not injure you in any way, except that (for I ought not lie to you or I would be doing an act of treachery) she wishes to have you in her power, and she wants to lay hold of your person so that even your heart is not at liberty."

"Very well," he said. "I am entirely willing. That will not pain me at all for I want to be in her prison." "So you will be, by my right hand which I lay on you! Now come, and in accordance with my advice conduct yourself so humbly that imprisonment may not turn out badly for you. Do not be alarmed at the prospect. I do not think that your detention will prove too onerous." The damsel then led him away, alarming him and then reassuring him and continuing to speak ambiguously about the prison in which he would be confined. No lover is really outside prison. She was right to call him a captive, for he who loves is indeed in prison.

The damsel took my Lord Ywain by the hand and led him to that place where he was held very dear although he feared greatly that he would be ill-received. It is not a wonder that he was fearful. They found the lady sitting on a red cushion. I warrant you that my Lord Ywain felt great timidity upon entering the chamber in which he found the lady, who did not utter a word to him. Because of this he experienced the greater terror and was prostrated because he thought that he had been betrayed. He stood apart for so long that the damsel spoke: "May the soul of her have five hundred curses who leads to the bower of a beautiful lady a knight who will not approach her and who does not have tongue or mouth or wits by which he can make himself known." With that word, she tugged him by the arm and said: "Come forward, Sir Knight, and do not be afraid that my lady will bite you, but beg her for peace and accord. I shall pray that she pardon you for the death of Esclados the Red, who was her lord."

My Lord Ywain then clasped his hands, fell on his knees, and spoke out like a true lover: "My Lady, truly I will not beg for mercy, but I will thank you for whatever you may wish to do with me, for nothing could be distasteful to me." "Indeed, Sir? What if I were to kill you?" "My Lady, by your

33

great mercy, you would not hear me protest it." "Never before," said she, "have I heard of such a thing. You have placed yourself wholly and completely at my disposal without being compelled to do so." "Lady, in truth, there is no power so great as that one which constrains me to submit altogether to your will. I am not afraid to do anything at all that it may please you to command. And if I could make amends for the slaying, in which respect I committed no wrong, I should atone for it without argument." "What!" said she. "Tell me, if you will be free of atonement, how it is that you did no wrong when you slew my lord?" "Lady," he replied; "by your mercy, when your lord attacked me what wrong did I do in defending myself? If a man, while defending himself, kills that one who seeks to slay or capture him, tell me if he has in any way committed a crime?" "By no means. Moreover, I think it would have been of no avail had I caused you to be slain. Yet, I would very much like to know what impulse leads you to agree altogether without protest to my will. I absolve you of all offenses and all misdeeds. But please sit down and tell me how it is you are so compliant. "My Lady," said he, "the impulse comes from my heart which has set itself on you. My heart, in fact, has put me in this frame of mind." "And what has so influenced your heart, fair sweet friend?" "My Lady, my eyes." "And what has influenced your eyes?" "The great beauty I see in you." "And how is beauty at fault?" "Because, Lady, it causes me to love so much." "Love? Love whom?" "You, dear Lady." "Me?" "Truly." "Indeed? How much?" "To this extent, that it could not be greater; in such a way that my heart will not turn from you nor will you find it elsewhere; to such a degree that I can think of nothing else; that I give myself wholly to you; that I love you more than myself; and that, if it please you, I would gladly live or die for your sake." "And would you dare undertake to defend my spring?" "Certainly, my Lady, against all men." "You may take it, then, that we are reconciled."

Thus they have quickly reached an agreement. And the lady, having before this announced a parliament to her barons, said: "Now we shall go forth to this hall where my people sit who have advised and counseled me in the emergency they foresaw and who authorize me to take a husband. And, in the face of the need, I shall do so. Here, then, I give myself to you, for I ought not refuse to take as lord a good knight and the son of a king."

Now the damsel had fully accomplished what she hoped to bring about. Moreover, my Lord Ywain was a better man than one could describe. The lady led him away with her into the hall which was full of knights and men-at-arms. My Lord Ywain was of such noble presence that all gazed on him with wonder and arose before him and greeted and bowed to him thinking: "This is the man whom my lady will take. May anyone who objects be cursed, for he appears to be a wonderfully fine man. Indeed, the Empress of Rome would find him a worthy husband. Would that he could plight his troth to her and she to him with her own hand and that he would wed her today or tomorrow." Thus they all spoke, one after the other. At the end of the hall the lady sat on a bench where all could see her. My Lord Ywain indicated that he intended to sit at her feet, but she caused him to rise. She then ordered her seneschal to make an announcement and that he speak so that he might be heard by all. The seneschal began at once, for he was neither disobedient nor stuttering: "Lords," said he, "war is now upon us. Every day the King is preparing hastily and to the best of his ability in order to come and lay waste our lands. Before two weeks have passed, all will have been devastated unless a good defender is available. Not as many as seven years have passed since our lady married, and she did so on your advice. Her lord is now dead and this distresses her. But he who held all this realm and adorned it so well now possesses only six feet of earth. It is a great pity that he lived so short a time. A woman is not able to bear a shield or fight with lance. It would advantage her and be most timely if she could marry a good lord. Never before was there a greater need. We all advise that she take a lord and not permit the custom to lapse which has been observed in this town for more than sixty years."

After this speech, all present said that it seemed proper to agree to this, and very soon they came to her feet. They urged her to act according to her wish, and she allowed herself to be supplicated until she agreed, as if against her will, to that which she would have done even if everyone had opposed her. She said: "Lords, since it is pleasing to you, this knight who is seated beside me has assiduously entreated me and asked for my hand. He wishes to devote himself to my honor and service, and I am grateful to him for that, and you should thank him too. I have not made his acquaintance before, to be sure, but I have heard tell of him. This worthy man, heed it well, is the son of King Urien. Quite apart from his being of noble family, he is a man of such great valor and is possessed of such courtesy and wisdom that I ought not be dissuaded. It seems to me that you all must have heard about my Lord Ywain and this is he who petitions for me. This man would be a more worthy lord on the wedding day than befits me."

Then all said: "This day shall not pass, if you act wisely, without your having celebrated the wedding. For the person who delays by one hour to act according to his advantage is very foolish." They pled so hard that she granted to them that which she would have done anyway. For Love commanded her to do the thing about which she sought advice and counsel. But she was accorded her wish with the greatest honor by reason of having the advice of her people. Their petitions did not pain her in any way; rather, they incited and urged on her heart to act in keeping with her desire. A horse, even when proceeding at a good rate, exerts himself the more when one spurs him on. Before all her barons the lady bestowed herself on my Lord Ywain. He took from the hand of her chaplain the Lady Laudine of Landuc, daughter of Duke Laudunet, about whom a lai is sung. That same day, without delay, he wed her and they celebrated their nuptials. Mitres and croziers were there in large numbers, for the lady had summoned her bishops and abbots. Joy and happiness reigned there and there was a great crowd and an immense display of wealth, more than I could describe to you even if I were to think about it a long time. It is better to remain silent than to speak inadequately. But now my Lord Ywain was master and the dead man wholly forgotten. The man who killed him was married to the widow and they slept together, and the people loved and valued the living lord more than they ever did the dead one.

The people served him well at the wedding celebration which lasted up to the day before the King with his entourage approached the miracle of the spring and the stone. Very nearly all his household were on this expedition; scarcely one remained at home. My Lord Kay said: "Ah! What has become of Ywain, for he did not return, he who boasted after feasting that he would set out to avenge his cousin? Clearly, that was after the wine. He has fled, I would guess. He would not have dared put in an appearance for anything. He talked much out of his great pride. That man is very bold who dares boast of what another would not praise him for. He has no witness to his prowess unless it be that of false flattery. Between a cowardly and a valiant man is a great difference, for the craven one near the fire speaks great words about himself, considering all men to be fools, and believing that no one will know the truth about him. But the brave man would endure considerable anguish if he heard someone relate the deeds of prowess he had performed. And yet it suits the coward well and he is not wrong if he praises himself and boasts, for he will find no one else who would lie for him. If he does not speak, who would speak for him? All would be silent, even the heralds who cry out the names of the valiant and disregard the weaklings."

My Lord Kay spoke thus, whereupon my Lord Gawain

remarked: "Enough my Lord Kay, enough! Although Ywain is not here, you do not know what obstacle he has met. Indeed, he has never abased himself to speak evil of you, but rather he has shown courtesy." "Sir," said Kay, "I shall be quiet. You will not hear me talk more about it today, for I see that it offends you." Then the King, in order to witness the storm, poured the basin full of water over the stone beneath the pine tree, and soon it rained torrentially. Then it was not a lengthy wait before my Lord Ywain entered the forest in arms without pausing and spurring at a gait faster than a gallop on a great stout horse that was strong, hardy, and swift. My Lord Kay resolved to request the combat, for, whatever the outcome, he always wanted to be the first to begin battles and encounters; otherwise, he would be very angry. In the presence of all he called to the King to grant him this duel. "Kay," said the King, "since it would please you and since you have requested it before all the others, it ought not be refused you."

Kay thanked him and then mounted. Now, if my Lord Ywain could bring down a little shame on him it would please him and he would do it gladly, for he recognized him well by his arms. He held up his shield by the straps, as Kay did his, and the two rushed at each other, spurring their mounts and lowering their lances which they held tightly. They thrust them forward somewhat so that they gripped them by the leather-wrapped handles. Upon crashing together, they took pains to deliver such blows that both lances were shattered and splintered as far back as the hand holds, but my Lord Ywain laid on a blow so powerful that he made Kay somersault out of his saddle and strike the ground head first. Not wishing to inflict greater injury, my Lord Ywain then dismounted and took the horse. This was pleasing to many and a number of them were prompted to remark: "Oh, how you are fallen, you who were arrogant toward others! Yet, it is only just that you be excused this time for such a thing has not happened to you before."

Meanwhile, my Lord Ywain approached the King leading the horse by the bridle because he wished to surrender him, and he spoke: "Sire, please accept this horse, for I should be doing wrong to keep anything belonging to you." "And who are you?" said the King. "I would not be able to recognize you in months if I were not to hear your name or to see you without your armor." Then my Lord Ywain admitted his name and Kay, overwhelmed with humiliation, was dejected, faint, and discomfited, for he had said that Ywain had taken to flight. But the rest were very happy and felt great joy over Ywain's success. Further, the King displayed great pleasure as did my Lord Gawain, a hundred times more than any other man. For he esteemed Ywain's company more than that of any knight he knew. The King requested him, if he would, to relate what had happened to him, for he had a great desire to know about the entire adventure. He begged him, then, to tell the whole story. Thereupon Ywain told them about the service and the good offices which the damsel had rendered him. He was never at a loss for a word nor did he forget anything. Afterwards he prayed the King that he and all his retinue would come and stay with him. They would bring him honor and happiness if they would take up lodgings there. The King replied that he would be happy to confer the honor, the joy, and the companionship of his presence for as much as eight days altogether, and my Lord Ywain expressed his gratitude. They delayed no longer but mounted and proceeded along the road to the city. My Lord Ywain sent ahead of the company a squire with a crane-hunting falcon in order that they might not surprise the lady and so that her people might bedeck their houses before the King's appearance. When the lady got the news of the King's approach, she was highly pleased nor did anyone hear the tidings who was not happy and elated. The lady summoned all together and requested that they go out to meet him, and they did not remonstrate or grumble because they wanted very much to carry out her wish.

39

They set out to meet the King of Britain on great Spanish horses and greeted very reverently first King Arthur and then his entire escort. "Welcome," they said, "to this company which is composed of such valiant men! Blessed be he who leads them and who brings us such splendid guests." In preparation for the King, the city resounded as the inhabitants gave expression to their joy. Silken draperies were brought out and hung for decoration, and they spread the roadway with rugs and hung others along the streets for the expected approach of the King. They made still another preparation, for against the heat of the sun they roofed the street with curtains. Church bells, horns, and trumpets made the town reverberate so that one could not have heard God's thunder. Maidens danced ahead of him; flutes, pipes, tambourines, cymbals, and drums were sounded. Nimble youths who leapt about likewise played their part, and all gave themselves up to jubilation. In this state of happiness they received the King just as they ought to do. The lady likewise came forward arrayed in imperial dress, consisting of a costume of new ermine and a diadem adorned entirely with rubies. Her countenance was by no means distressed; rather it was so gay and so radiant that, in my opinion, she was more beautiful than any goddess.

The crowd surged about her and the people said, one after the other: "Welcome to the King, the lord of kings and of the nobility of the world!" Before the King could make any response to them he saw the lady coming toward him apparently with the intention of holding his stirrup. Since he did not wish to permit this, he hastened to dismount as soon as he glimpsed her. She greeted him and spoke: "Welcome a hundred thousand times to the King, my lord, and may his nephew Gawain be blessed." "To your fair person and your countenance, beautiful creature, happiness and good fortune!" said the King. Then like a noble and gracious man, the King clasped her about the waist and she embraced him in her arms. I shall not report the other speeches with which she welcomed him, but no one ever heard tell of any people so nobly welcomed and so honored and received.

I could tell you a great deal about their happiness if I chose to waste my words, but I want only to make a brief allusion to the acquaintance struck up by the sun and moon in a private encounter. Do you know about whom I intend to speak? Of that man who was chief of knights and who was renowned above all others and who ought indeed to be called the sun. I speak of my Lord Gawain, for all chivalry was made illustrious by his example just as the morning sun sends forth its rays and spreads light in all places where it shines. And further I call that other one the moon who can be nothing other than a person of great prudence and courtesy. Yet I do not so call her because of her good repute, but also because she was Lunete by name. The damsel was called Lunete and she was a handsome brunette, very discreet, shrewd, and intelligent. When she made herself known to my Lord Gawain, he prized and loved her greatly and called her his sweetheart. Because she had saved his comrade and friend from death, he offered her his service. And she related and explained to him with what difficulty she had contended with her mistress to the end that she took my Lord Ywain for her husband and how she protected him from the hands of those people who searched for him and how he was in their midst although they failed to see him. My Lord Gawain laughed a great deal at what she related to him saying: "Damsel I place myself at your service, such a knight as I am, whether or not you should ever have need of me. Do not by any means overlook me if you think I can ever be of aid to you. I am yours and you are from this time on my own damsel." "Thank you, Sir," said she.

While these two were becoming acquainted, others indulged in tender exchanges. For there were some ninety ladies present, each of whom was handsome, well-mannered, noble, sophisticated, prudent, and wise, a person of high lineage. Thus, the newcomers were delighted to embrace and kiss them and to engage in conversation and gaze on them while they were seated beside them: so much pleasure at least they had from them. My Lord Ywain was gratified that the King was staying with him. The lady honored them so much one and all that to a fool it might have appeared that the services she rendered arose from actual love for them on her part. But such people should be considered simple-minded who think that when a lady is polite and converses with some miserable man, making him happy and embracing him, that she is in love with him. A silly person is made happy by pleasant speech and is greatly diverted by it. All of them devoted themselves wholly to pleasure throughout the week. Those who wished found great sport hunting in the forest and in falconry, and whoever wished to see the realm which my Lord Ywain had taken possession of along with the lady whom he married undertook to visit castles located within a distance of two, three, or four leagues.

When the King had finished his visit and wished to remain no longer, he prepared to take up his journey. But during that week his people had implored and urged him as strongly as they could that they take my Lord Ywain with them. "What? Will you be one of those men," said my Lord Gawain to Ywain, "who are worth the less because of their wives? May that man be shamed by Saint Mary who weds only to deteriorate! Whoever takes a mistress or wife ought to be the better for a beautiful lady, for it is not fitting that she love him if his valor and fame are left behind. Indeed, you yourself would become angry at Love if you were to degenerate. A woman soon repudiates her love, and she is right in so doing, for she will prize little a man who in any way demeans himself after he has become master of her realm. Now, above all, should your reputation increase! Slip your bridle and halter and let us, you and me, engage in tournaments lest people consider you a jealous man. You should not day dream but rather seek out tournaments, accept combat, and joust vigorously whatever the cost to you. He who indulges a great deal in dreaming gets nowhere. Indeed, it is fitting that you come along for I shall be under your banner. See to it, fair comrade, that our fellowship does not fail on your account, for it will certainly not fail because of me. It is a marvel how a person longs for comfort the whole of his life. When postponed, the pleasures of life become the sweeter. There is more delight in tasting a mild pleasure after it has been delayed than in partaking of a great one at once. The joy one finds in a love which comes late seems like green wood when set afire, for it will give out more heat and will retain it longer the more one delays burning it. When one becomes accustomed to something, he finds it very difficult to foresake it; even when he wishes he finds that he cannot do it. I do not at all speak as if I had as beautiful a lady as you have, my dear companion. By the faith which I owe to God and his saints, I would leave such a lady very reluctantly. In my opinion, in fact, I would be Love's fool. But a man who does not know how to govern himself may well advise another, just like those preachers who, although disloyal hypocrites, teach and prattle about righteousness which they themselves have no intention of respecting."

My Lord Gawain continued to speak about such matters imploring him so much that he promised that he would speak to his lady and that he would go off with him if he could obtain her leave. Whether in so doing he would be foolish or wise, he would not depart without securing her permission to return to Britain. He then conferred with his wife, who was not prepared for the favor he intended to ask, saying: "My dearest wife, you who are my heart and soul, my delight, my happiness, and my well-being, grant me one boon for your honor and for mine!" The lady acceded without understanding what it was he wished to ask for: "Fair Sir, you may ask me for any favor you wish." Then my Lord Ywain begged her for permission to accompany the King and to engage in tourneying so that no one could call him a coward. She said: "I grant you leave for a certain period of time, but the love

I have for you will certainly turn to hate should you remain away beyond the time I shall designate. Understand that I will not break my word; even if you break yours, I will still keep mine. If you wish to keep my love and hold nothing more dear, remember to return by all means within a year at least—that is, by the eighth day after the Feast of Saint John, for today is the octave of that Feast. You will be cast out and deprived of my love if you are not with me on that day."

My Lord Ywain lamented, sighed deeply, and was scarcely able to speak because of pain: "My Lady, this period would be too long. If I were a dove, I would fly to your side whenever I wished. And I pray God, if it please him, that he will not detain me for so long a time. Still, a man may intend to come back at once although he is not aware what the future may hold for him. Nor can I know what will happen to me, for mishaps of illness or imprisonment may restrain me. You impose too great a penalty if you do not at least make allowance for unavoidable delay."

"Sir," she said, "I shall take that possibility into account. And yet, I solemnly assure you that, if God preserves you from death, no obstacles will detain you so long as you bear me in mind. Now, slip on your finger this ring which I am lending you. I shall explain to you fully about the stone: No true and devoted lover will remain in prison nor will he lose blood or undergo any other harm if he wears this and holds it dear and keeps his beloved in mind. Rather, he will become more durable than iron. This will serve you as shield and hauberk. I have never surrendered or lent it to any knight before, but because of my love I give it to you."

Now Sir Ywain asked permission to go, yet he sorrowed much at his leave-taking. The King, however, did not wish to tarry for anything that one might say to him. Accordingly, he waited only until all the palfreys were led forth caparisoned and harnessed. It was done entirely as he wished: they brought forth the palfreys and there was left only to mount them. I do not know whether I ought to relate to you in what manner Ywain took his departure, of the kisses rained on him mixed with tears and flavored with sweetness. And what shall I reveal to you about the King? How the lady with her maidens and knights convoyed him? I would pause too long over this task. When the lady wept, the King urged her to stop and return to her household. He implored her so strongly that, in great distress, she turned about and led her people home with her. My Lord Ywain was so deeply pained upon leaving the lady that he left his heart behind. The King was able to lead off his body, but by no means could he carry away his heart as well. For she who remained at home held and joined herself so closely to that heart that he did not have the strength to draw it away. The body cannot live without the heart. At any rate, if the body ever maintained life without a heart, no man ever saw that marvel. Nevertheless, such a miracle now came about, for Ywain continued to live on without his heart which his body had previously enclosed. His heart had a good hostelry, however, and his body lived in hopes of its return. Thus, he made a heart of strange fashion out of hope, which often plays the traitor and is false. Indeed, I believe that he could not know the hour at which hope would desert him.

If he were to exceed by a single day the period which had been agreed to, he would hardly be able to win a truce and peace with his lady. But, as I expected, he tarried beyond his time, for my Lord Gawain would not permit him to leave. Together, the two attended tournaments wherever they were held. As the year passed, my Lord Ywain performed so well that my Lord Gawain was at pains to honor him and caused him to remain so long that the entire year elapsed and enough of the next so that mid-August arrived. At that time the King held court at Chester, and there they arrived after a tournament in which my Lord Ywain had engaged and carried off all the glory.

The tale goes on to relate, I believe, that the two companions did not choose to lodge in the town; rather, they

45

caused their tent to be pitched outside town and held court there. They did not go to the King's court; instead, the King attended theirs, for with them were the best knights in the largest numbers. King Arthur came to sit among them, when Ywain suddenly bethought himself. Since the time he had taken leave of his lady he had not been so much dismayed as on this occasion. For he now realized that he had broken his pledge and exceeded his period of absence. He held back his tears with difficulty, and it was only out of shame that he succeeded. While still lost in thought, he saw a damsel bearing down at a great pace on a black and white palfrey. She dismounted before the pavilion, no one assisting her to get down and no one advancing to take her horse. As soon as she caught sight of the King, she let her cloak fall and unencumbered she entered the tent and presented herself before the King. She announced that her mistress sent greetings to the King and my Lord Gawain and to all others except Ywain, the disloyal one, the traitor, liar, and cheat. He had misled and deceived her. She had clearly experienced the treachery of that one who pretended to be a true lover, but he was a villain, an impostor, and thief. "This robber has imposed on my lady, who did not anticipate such evil, and she did not believe that he would steal away her heart. Those who love truly do not steal hearts, yet one may properly call those thieves who make a pretense of love but who know nothing about it. The true lover takes the heart of his beloved, to be sure, but he does not steal it away. Rather, he guards it lest thieves, in the semblance of honorable men, rob her of it. Such men are hypocritical and treacherous thieves who exert themselves to steal the affections of those they do not really care for. The true lover, wherever he goes, holds dear his beloved's heart and returns it to her. But Ywain has slain my lady, although she had expected that he would treasure her heart and come back again with it before the year elapsed. Ywain, now were you most negligent! You could not remember that you were to return to my lady within a year. She gave you respite up to the Feast of Saint John, and yet you held her in such scorn that never since have you thought of this agreement. My lady has marked in her chamber each day and each season. For, whoever is in love is in great sorrow and is unable to sleep soundly. Instead, the whole night long he counts and figures the days as they come and go. Do you realize how lovers behave? They take account of the time and seasons. Her complaint is not unreasonable nor is it premature. I do not voice it merely to raise an uproar, but I say this much: that we have been deceived by the man who wed my lady. Ywain, my lady holds no affection for you, but through me orders you never to return to her, nor may you any longer keep her ring! She commands that you send it back by me whom you see before you. Surrender it, for you are bound to do so!"

Ywain was unable to reply because he was bereft of reason and speech. The damsel stepped forward and took the ring from his finger, then she commended the King to God and all the others as well save for the one whom she left in deep grief. His chagrin increased within him. Whatever he heard added to his burden; whatever he saw distressed him. He would have preferred to take to flight all alone in so wild a land that no one would know where to seek him and where there was no man or woman, and no person would know any more about him than as if he were sunk in an abyss. He hated nothing so much as himself, nor did he know to whom he could turn for comfort in the death that he faced. He would have preferred madness if he could not wreak vengeance on himself, since he had destroyed his own happiness. He absented himself from the barons for he feared he would go out of his senses in their presence. But, taking no heed of him, they permitted him to depart alone. They knew well that he had no interest in their talk or their company. And he kept on his way until he had left the pavilions far behind.

Then there burst out a storm in his mind so severe that he went mad. He clawed and tore at himself and fled across plains and fields and left his people bewildered, and they wondered where he could have gone. They set out in search of him throughout the countryside, in the lodgings of knights, in the hedgerows, and in the orchards, but they looked for him where he was not to be found. Still in flight, he continued until near a park he came upon a boy with a bow and five feathered arrows which were very sharp and broad-headed. He had sufficient sense to go to the boy and take from him the bow and arrows, which he held. But of what he did, he remembered nothing afterwards. Then he lay in ambush in the forest for wild animals and killed them and ate their flesh raw.

In the wilderness he dwelt much like a lunatic or a wild man until he came up to the very humble and meager abode of a hermit. The hermit himself was grubbing in his field, but when he saw a naked man he realized immediately that the man did not have all his wits, and this he understood very clearly. Out of apprehension, he shut himself in his hut. Yet, because of his charity, that worthy man set some bread and some pure water outside his dwelling on a narrow window ledge. The other approached. He longed for the bread, and seized it and chewed it up. I do not believe that he had ever tasted anything so strong and bitter. The measure of barley kneaded together with the straw of which the bread, more sour than yeast, was made could not have cost so much as five sous. Moreover, the bread was mouldy and as dry as bark. But hunger tormented and afflicted him so much that the bread tasted like a sauce to him. For hunger is a sauce, well blended and well suited to all foods. My Lord Ywain ate the hermit's bread, which seemed palatable to him, and drank the cold water from the pot. When he had eaten, he reëntered the forest and hunted bucks and does. And the good man under the roof, when he saw him leave prayed God to protect and watch over him lest he should ever come again to those parts. But there is no creature, however little reason he has, who does not return very eagerly to the place where he has been well treated. Thus, a whole day did not pass while he was in this madness that Ywain did not carry some wild game to the hermit's door. This was the life he led, and the good man undertook to skin the animals and cook sufficient of the meat. And every day he set out bread and the pot of water by the window for the sustenance of the mad man. Thus, Ywain had meat without salt and pepper and cold water from a spring for food and drink. And the good man took steps to sell the hides and to buy bread made of barley or oats or other grain, and thus he had all necessities—bread and meat in plenty, which sufficed him for a long period.

Finally one day, two damsels and their lady, in whose service they were, found Ywain sleeping in the forest. When they glimpsed the naked man, one of the three dismounted and ran up to inspect him closely in order to learn whether anything about him would permit her to identify him. She gazed at him attentively and would have recognized him at once had he been in rich attire, as he had been on many an occasion. But she was slow to recognize him and continued her examination of all points until at last she noticed a scar on his face. My Lord Ywain, she knew well, had such a scar on his face. She had seen it frequently, and because of this she perceived that it was he without any doubt. But it was wholly a marvel how it came about that she found him destitute and naked. She crossed herself often and wondered greatly, but she did not touch or awaken him. Instead, she took her horse, remounted, and returned to the others, and weeping reported her experience. I do not know whether I should tell you all the sadness she exhibited, but still sobbing she told her mistress: "Lady, I have found Ywain, the knight who of the whole world is proved the best and the most adorned with virtues. I do not know what evils have befallen this gentleman. I think he must have suffered some grief which caused him thus to abase himself, for one can go insane from woe. One may recognize and see that he is not at all rational, for it would never happen that he would act so ignobly had he not lost his wits. Now, would that God restore his mind to him as good as ever and moreover that it would please him to come to your aid. For Count Aliers who makes war on you has inflicted too much harm on you. I would see the conflict between you two ended to your great honor if God were to give you such good fortune that Ywain were to regain his senses and undertake to help you in this extremity."

The lady said: "Now, have a care. For indeed, if he does not take to flight, I suspect that we can, with God's help, cure him of all the madness and confusion in his mind. But it is necessary that we go back, for I recall an ointment given to me by Morgan the Wise. She told me that there is no derangement of the mind that it will not cure."

They immediately proceeded to the town which was near at hand. Indeed, it was not farther off than a half-league—in terms of the leagues they have in that country, for in comparison, two of ours make one of theirs, and four make two. Ywain remained there by himself asleep while the women set out to fetch the ointment. Unlocking her chest, the lady drew from it a box which she entrusted to the damsel, begging her not to be too liberal with it. She should rub the temples and forehead with it, for there was no need to use it elsewhere. She should apply it only to the temples and conserve the remainder because, except for the mind, there was nothing amiss with him. She also had the maiden take him a fur cloak, a coat, and a mantle of scarlet. These the maiden carried with her and she also led by her right hand a very good palfrey. Moreover, she added a shirt, fine-spun breeches, and new hose, well cut, from her own possessions. She started at once and found Ywain still asleep where she had left him. Placing her horse in a thicket and tethering him well, she approached the place where he slept with the clothing and the medicine. She showed great hardihood in walking up to the mad man so close that she could touch and minister to him. Taking the salve, she massaged him with it until none at all was left in the box. She wished for his recovery so strongly that she applied the medicine everywhere, expending the whole of it, for she did not heed her mistress's warning nor did she even remember it. She used more than was required but she considered that she employed it in a good cause. She rubbed his temples and forehead and the whole body down to the toe. She anointed his temples and his entire body so much that in the heat of the sun the madness and melancholy passed out of his brain altogether. Yet, it was foolish of her to apply the salve to his body; there was no need for that. If she had had five measure of the medicine, however, I believe that she would have used it all. She then gathered up the box and ran off and concealed herself near her horse. But she did not take the clothing away with her because, should God restore him to his senses, she hoped that, seeing the apparel, he would take it and dress himself.

She remained behind a great oak tree until he had slept sufficiently and was cured, refreshed, and again in possession of his reason and memory. But, noticing that he was as naked as ivory, he was deeply embarrassed, and he would have been still more so had be known the whole truth of his experience. But he knew no more than that he found himself naked. Seeing before him the fresh clothing, he wondered greatly how and by what chance it came to be there. But, grieved and perturbed by his nudity, he said that he would be dead and betrayed if anyone at all should come upon him thus and recognize him. At once he dressed himself and peered into the forest to see whether he could glimpse any person. He resolved to rise and stand, but he was not equal to the exertion and thus could not leave. It was necessary that he find help, someone to aid and lead him. For his grave illness had so affected him that for no reward could he have remained on his feet. Thereupon the damsel, deciding to hesitate no longer, mounted and rode close by him as though she did not know about his presence. And that one, who stood in great need of help so that it did not matter to him who might conduct him to some hostelry where he might regain his strength, exerted himself to call out loudly.

The damsel then looked about her as if she did not know what it was. As if surprised, she went here and there, for she did not want to go straight up to him. He commenced to call out again: "Damsel! This way! This way!" And the damsel turned her ambling palfrey in his direction. By such a trick she made him think that she knew nothing about him and had never seen him before, and thus she displayed tact and courtesy. "Sir Knight, what do you want that you call out to me with such urgency?" "Ah!" said he. "Wise damsel, I find myself here in this forest by what mischance I do not understand. For God's sake and your own faith, I beg that you turn over to me as a loan or give me outright this palfrey which you are leading." "Willingly, Sir. But come with me to the place where I am going." "Where?" he asked. "To a town a little beyond this forest." "Damsel, now tell me whether you might have any employment for me?" "Yes," said she. "But I believe that you are not entirely well. You ought to rest for at least fifteen days. Take this horse which I am leading in my right hand, and we will go to the hostelry." And he, who did not ask for more, took it and mounted, and they set out until they came to a bridge over a stream which was rushing and roaring. The damsel cast into it the empty box which she was carrying, having decided to excuse herself to her mistress with respect to the ointment as follows: she would say that in crossing the bridge she had the misfortune to drop the box from her hand when her palfrey lurched with her. But if she herself had fallen after it, the loss would have been even greater. This lie she intended to tell when she came before her lady.

Together they continued on their way until they arrived at the castle where the lady amiably detained my Lord Ywain while she inquired confidentially of her damsel about the box of ointment. The damsel told the falsehood just as she had rehearsed it for she did not dare tell the truth. The

52

lady then fell into a great rage, saying: "This is a very painful loss, and I am perfectly sure that it will never be recovered. Yet, when a thing is gone, one can only resign himself. One always believes that he desires for his good something which later turns out to be evil. Thus I, who expected to get some good and some satisfaction from this vassal, have forfeited the best and choicest of my possessions. Nevertheless, I must ask you to attend to him in all ways." "Now, my Lady, you say well. For it would be too great a shame to turn a single mischance into a double sorrow."

They then kept silent about the box and in whatever ways they could and were able they made my Lord Ywain comfortable. They bathed him and washed his head, and caused him to be shaved and clipped, for one could have gathered up a whole handful of hair on his face. There was nothing he wished for that was not done for him. If he wanted arms, someone arranged to provide them; if he wanted a horse, one awaited him, handsome and large, strong and hardy. Ywain remained until, on a certain Tuesday, Count Alier came to the town with knights and men-at-arms and set fires and pillaged. The people of the town arose and provided themselves with weapons. Then, armed and unarmed, they sallied forth to meet the plunderers who did not flee at their approach but awaited them in a defile.

My Lord Ywain struck into the press, for he had rested for so long a time that his strength had returned. He battered a knight's shield with such force that he knocked the knight and his horse together in a heap, I believe. That man never got up again, for his heart was crushed in his body and his spine was broken. My Lord Ywain drew back a little, then attacked again. Covering himself completely with his shield, he rushed forward in order to clear the defile. One could not have counted one, two, three, four as quickly as he could be seen to strike down four knights promptly and with dispatch. Those who were with him derived great courage from his example. If one of poor and cowardly heart sees a brave man undertake a great enterprise, a sense of shame and odium will seize upon and expel the timid heart in his body and give him at once a brave and resolute heart. Thus, those men became valiant and each of them held his place in the mêlée and the attack very well. The lady in the tower of her castle raised on high saw the fray and the assault succeed in gaining possession of the defile and she observed lying on the ground a sufficient number of wounded and dead, both of her men and the enemy but more of the others than of hers. For the courteous, valiant, and competent Lord Ywain had forced them to cry mercy, just as the falcon does the teal.

Those men and women enclosed in the castle watched the battle saying: "Ah, how brave a fighter! How he makes his adversaries yield! How fiercely he attacks them! He sets on them like a lion on a doe when need and hunger spur him on. All our other knights are the more hardy and gallant because of him. Indeed, were it not for him alone, no lance would be splintered nor any sword drawn for striking. A valorous man deserves to be loved and cherished when he is to be found. See now how he proves himself; see how he maintains the battle order; see how he stains with blood his lance and naked sword; see how he presses them; see how he pursues them, how he comes at them, how he passes by them, how he turns about, how he comes back. Yet, he wastes small time in whirling about and delays little in returning to the attack. See how he enters into the thick of battle, how he prizes his shield very slightly, allowing it to be cut up without any regard for it at all. See how eager he is to avenge the strokes given to him. If someone were to make lances of all the forest of Argonne, I believe that he would not have any left by nightfall. For one cannot place so many in the lance-rest that he could not shatter them all and ask for still more. And see how he wields the sword whenever he draws it. Roland with Durendal did not bring about such devastation among the Turks in Ronceval or in Spain. If Ywain had in his troop any companions so effective as he, the wretch whom we deplore would depart in distress or remain only to be destroyed."

They remarked further that any woman would be fortunate to be loved by one so potent in arms and so distinguished above all just as a taper among candles, the moon among the stars, and the sun above the moon. He had gained the heart of this one and that one so that all hoped that, because of the prowess they observed in him, he would betake himself to the lady and that the realm would be under his governance.

Everybody praised him and they spoke the truth in so doing. For those he overcame contended with each other in flight. But he pursued them closely and all his companions with him, who felt as secure in his presence as if enclosed by a high, thick wall of hard stone. The chase continued so long that those who fled became weary and their pursuers cut them to pieces and disemboweled their horses. The living rolled over the dead bodies and injured and killed each other. Savagely they attacked. Meanwhile the count took to his heels and my Lord Ywain, who was not reluctant to follow, trailed him. The count traveled so far that he reached the foot of a high mound and was near the entrance of a strong fortress which belonged to him. At that point the count was halted and there was no one nearby able to assist him. Without negotiating for too long a time, my Lord Ywain received his surrender. For, when the count held up his hands and the two were by themselves man to man, there was no chance of escape, or evasion, or of further defense for him. Therefore, the count swore that he would render himself up to the Lady of Noroison and accept imprisonment and make peace on her terms. And when he had given his word, Ywain made him uncover his head, remove the shield from about his neck, and hand over his bare sword. The honor of leading the count away a prisoner was due to him, and he turned him over to his enemies who made no little joy. The news was reported at the castle before their arrival. All came out to meet them, the lady before all the rest. My Lord Ywain took the prisoner by the hand and presented him to her. The count agreed completely to her wishes and demands and affirmed the agreement by his word, by oath, and by sureties. He gave pledges and swore to her that he would keep the peace all his days and that he would make good her losses, whatever she could demonstrate by proof. And he would also provide new houses in place of those he had razed to the ground.

When these things were settled just as was pleasing to the lady, my Lord Ywain requested permission to depart. She would not have granted him leave had he desired to take her as mistress or marry her. He would not permit anyone to follow or accompany him a single step of his way but left promptly, and no appeal to him was of any avail. He took up his journey and left the lady, to whom he had brought great joy, greatly discomfited. For the more intense the pleasure he had given her the more was she made sad and distressed when he did not choose to remain longer. She had hoped to honor him and, had it been pleasing to him, would have made him lord of whatever she owned, or else she would have given him for his services a sum of money as great as he would wish to take with him. But he would listen no longer to the arguments of man or woman. From the knights and the lady, even though it was painful to them, he departed and would not permit himself to be detained further.

My Lord Ywain proceeded thoughtfully through a deep forest until he heard a loud, sorrowful outcry in the thicket. He turned toward the noise he had heard, and when he reached it he saw in a clearing a lion and a dragon. The dragon was holding the lion by the tail and was scorching his flanks with his flaming breath. My Lord Ywain did not stand watching this marvel for long, but he considered which of the two he should aid. Then he determined that he should aid the lion because one so venomous and wicked as a dragon ought not escape harm. The dragon was poisonous; fire shot forth from his mouth, so full of evil was he. Therefore, my Lord

Ywain resolved to kill him first. He drew his sword, approached closer, and held his shield before his face so that he would not be injured by the flame from the dragon's throat, which was larger than a pot. Should the lion attack him next, he would not fail to have a fight. But, whatever should happen thereafter, he was committed to help him now. Pity itself urged him on and impelled him to offer succor and aid to the noble and honorable beast. With his sword, which cut clean, he attacked the evil dragon, slicing him in two right down to the ground. He struck again and again so many times that he minced and hacked him into small bits. But he was obliged to shear off a piece of the lion's tail because the head of the vile dragon was still fastened to it. Only so much as was necessary he cut off; he could not have removed less of it.

When he had rescued the lion, he thought that it would be necessary to defend himself if he were to set upon him, but the lion did not serve him so. Hear what the lion did instead: He conducted himself like a free-born and well-mannered man. Acting as though offering submission to Ywain, he stood upright on his two hind feet and, with forepaws joined and extended, he bowed his head to the ground. Then he kneeled and his face was moist with tears of humility. My Lord Ywain knew for a truth that the lion was thanking him and humbling himself because he had slain the dragon and preserved him from death. He was greatly pleased with this adventure. He cleaned the poison and filth of the dragon from his sword, placed it again in the scabbard, and took up his journey. But the lion stayed by his side and never went away from him. Thereafter he was always in his presence, for he intended to serve and protect him.

He set out in front and went along until the wind brought him the smell of wild animals grazing. Then hunger and his own instinct summoned him to go hunting for food. Nature wanted him to do this. He followed the scent a little way until he had shown his lord that he had picked up the trail of some wild animal. Then he stopped and looked at him, for he wanted to serve him according to his wishes, and had no desire to go anywhere against his master's will. And Ywain could see from his expression that the lion was showing him that he was waiting for him. He plainly saw and fully understood that if he went no further the lion would do likewise, and that if he followed him the lion would capture the game he had smelled.

Then Ywain urged him on, just as he would have done with a hunting dog; and the lion immediately started to follow the scent; nor had he lied to him in any way, for he had not gone the distance of a bow-shot before he saw a roe-buck grazing all alone in a glen. Now the lion would catch it as he wished, and so he did at the first bound, and then drank its warm blood. When he had killed it, he threw it over his back, and carried it till he came before his master, who held him very dear from then on, and took him as his companion for all the days of his life, because of the great love that was in him.

It was already nearly nightfall, so he decided to camp there and skin as much of the roe-buck as he might wish to eat. Then he began to skin it; he split the hide under the rib, and took off a piece of larded meat from the loin. He drew fire from a flint and set a dry log on fire; then he put the meat on a spit so that it would cook swiftly in the fire, and he roasted it until it was cooked. But he got no pleasure from the meal, for there was neither bread nor wine nor salt, nor tablecloth, nor knife, nor anything else. While he ate, his lion lay before him and never moved, but rather watched him constantly until he had eaten so much of his meat that he could eat no more. Then the lion ate all that was left of the roe-buck, right down to the bones. Ywain rested his head all night on his shield, and had such repose as it afforded; and the lion had so much good sense that he stayed awake and took care to watch over the horse, grazing on the grass—which fattened it little.

In the morning they went off together, and such a life, it

seems to me, as they had led that night, they went on leading together for nearly all that week, until chance brought them to the fountain under the pine. There my Lord Ywain nearly went out of his mind again, when he approached the fountain, and the stone and the chapel. A thousand times he called himself unfortunate and sorrowful, and he fell down in a faint, so sorrowful was he; and his sword, which slid easily, fell from its sheath, and the point pierced the links of mail of his hauberk near the neck, beside his cheek. No link resisted, and the sword cut the skin of his neck beneath the white mail, and made the blood flow.

The lion thought he saw his companion and his lord lying dead before him. You never heard tell of any greater grief than what he then began to demonstrate! He writhed and clawed and cried out and wished to kill himself with the sword, which he believed had killed his lord. With his teeth he drew out the sword and leaned it on a log and braced it against the trunk of a tree behind, so that it would not turn aside when he struck it with his chest. His will would already have been accomplished, when Ywain recovered from his faint; and the lion braked his run—he had been running full speed toward death, just like a maddened boar that pays no heed to where it rushes.

In such a way did my Lord Ywain faint before the stone. When he came to he greatly blamed himself for the year which he had gone beyond and because of which his lady hated him, and he said: "Why does he not kill himself, this sorrowful creature who has taken joy from himself? What am I doing, then, if I do not kill myself? How can I stay here and see my lady's things? Why does my soul stay within my body? What is a soul doing in so sorrowful a body? If it had gone away, it would not be in such torment. I must truly hate and blame and despise myself, and truly so I do. He who loses joy and solace by his own misdeed and by his mistake must surely have a deadly hatred for himself. He must hate and kill himself; and I, while no one sees me, why do I spare myself and not kill myself? Have I not seen this lion who was so sad because of me that without delay he wanted to thrust my sword through his chest and into his body? And am I to fear death, I who changed my joy to sorrow? Joy has become a stranger to me.—Joy? What joy? I shall say no more of it, for no one could say this, and I have asked a very idle question. I was certain of the most joyous of joys, but it lasted only a very short time. And it is not right that he who loses this through his misdeed should ever have good fortune."

While Ywain was lamenting in this way, a sorrowful prisoner, who was closed inside the chapel, saw and heard this thing through a crack in the wall. As soon as he had gotten up from his faint, she called out to him: "God!" she cried, "what do I see there? Who is it that is so grievously distressed?" And he replied, "And who are you?" "I am," said she, "a prisoner, the saddest creature alive." He answered, "Be still, foolish creature! Such sorrow is joy! Such evil, goodness, compared to the evil from which I suffer. The more a man has learned to live in pleasure and in joy, the more he is lost and stupefied by sorrow, when it comes to him, than is another man; the weak man carries the burden, out of habit and being used to doing so, that another, of greater strength, would not carry for any thing." "In faith," said she, "I know well that what you say is true, but that does not convince me in the least that you are worse off than I am, and for this reason I do not believe it at all, for it seems to me that you can go wherever you wish, and I am imprisoned here. And my fate is such that tomorrow I shall be taken from here and put to death." "Oh, God!" said he, "for what crime?" "Sir Knight, may God never have mercy on my soul, if I have deserved it in any way! And nevertheless I shall tell you the truth, without any lie. I am here in this prison because I've been accused of treason, and I can't find anyone to defend me so that I won't be burned or hanged tomorrow."

"Now first," said he, "may I say that my sorrow and my

anguish go beyond your grief, for you could be delivered from this danger by anyone at all. Could this not be?" "Yes, but I don't know by whom: there are only two men in the world who would dare to engage in battle against three men in order to defend me." "What? By God, are there three of them, then?" "Yes, Sire, by my faith: they are three who accuse me of treason." "And who are those who love you so that one of them would be so bold as to dare to fight against three to save and protect you?" "I shall tell you truthfully: the one is my Lord Gawain and the other my Lord Ywain, because of whom I shall tomorrow be wrongfully put to death."

"Because of whom? What did you say?" "Sire, may God help me, because of the son of King Urien." "Now have I heard you clearly; but you will never die without him. I myself am that Ywain on account of whom you are so frightened, and you, I believe, are she who kept me in the room; you saved my life between the two sliding doors, where I was worried and sorrowful, alarmed and distressed. I should have been killed or captured there, had it not been for your good help. Now tell me, my sweet friend, who are these people who accuse you of treason, and have imprisoned you in this dungeon?"

"Sire, I shall keep it from you no longer, since it pleases you that I should tell you. It is true that I did not hesitate in the least to help you in good faith. On my recommendation my lady received you as her lord; she believed my advice and my counsel, and by the holy Pater noster, I believed, and still believe, I acted more for her advantage than for yours: so I can now reveal to you, I sought her honor and your will, God help me. But when it happened that you had overstayed the year, at the end of which you were to come back here to my lady, she became angry with me, and considered herself much deceived for having believed me. And when the seneschal learned this—he's a wicked man, a disloyal rogue, who was very envious of me because my lady believed me more

61

than him in many matters—he saw his chance to stir up great anger between her and me. Right in full court and in front of everyone he accused me of having betrayed her for you, and I had no counsel nor help apart from myself, and I knew that I had never done nor thought any treason against my lady. I replied like one who is terrified, immediately, taking no counsel, and said that I would have my cause defended by one knight against three. He was never so courteous as to deign to refuse, and I could not withdraw, no matter what happened. So he took me at my word, and I had to obtain the promise of a knight who would fight against three, within a delay of forty days. Then I went to many courts: I was at King Arthur's court, but there I found no one to advise me nor anyone who could tell me anything of you that pleased me, for they had no news of you."

"And what about my Lord Gawain, the noble, the kind, where then was he? No damsel in need of counsel ever failed to get help from him." "He would have made me happy and glad, if I had found him at court; he would never refuse anything I asked of him. But a knight had taken the Queen away, so I was told, and the King was out of his mind, to let her go away with him. I believe that Kay accompanied her to the knight who was to take here away, and now my Lord Gawain, who is looking for her, has undertaken a very difficult task. He will never have a day's rest until he has found her again. I have told you the whole truth of my misfortune. Tomorrow I shall die a shameful death; I shall be burned without delay, by your fault and out of spite."

And Ywain answered: "May it never please God that anyone would harm you in any way on my account; as long as I'm alive, you'll never die there! Tomorrow you can expect me to do all in my power to work for your deliverance, just as I ought to do. But don't go telling people who I am! Whatever may happen in the battle, be sure that no one recognizes me!"

"Sire, no torture would make me reveal your name. Rather

I would suffer death, since you wish it to be so. And yet I beg you not to come back here for me. I do not want you to undertake such a cruel combat. I thank you for the promise that you would gladly do it, but now be completely acquitted of it, for it is better that I alone die than that I see them rejoice at your death and at mine. For I would not escape after they had killed you; it is better that you remain alive than that we both die."

"Now you have said something very troubling, sweet friend," said my Lord Ywain. "Perhaps you do not really wish to be saved from death, or else you scorn the help I bring, to assist you. I do not wish to debate with you any longer, for you have done so much for me, to be sure, that I must not fail you in any need that you may have. I know full well that you are afraid, but, if it please God in whom I believe, they will all three be dishonored by this. Now, it only remains for me to go away somewhere, to seek lodging in this wood, for I know of no hostel near here."

"Sire," said she, "God grant you both lodging and good night, and keep you, as I wish, from any thing that troubles you."

My Lord Ywain then went away, and the lion was ever with him. They traveled until they came near to a strong refuge that belonged to a baron, closed all around by a wall thick and strong and high. The castle feared no assault by mangonel or catapult, for it was extremely strong; but outside the wall the open space was so razed that no hut nor house remained standing. You will learn the reason for this another time, when the moment is appropriate. My Lord Ywain went straight on toward the castle, and as many as seven pages jumped up, and lowered a bridge for him, and went out to meet him. But they were greatly afraid of the lion, which they saw coming with him, and they asked him, please, to leave his lion at the door, so that he would not wound or kill them. And he replied, "Do not suggest such a thing, for never will I come in without him: either we will both receive lodging,

63

or I shall stay out here, for I love him as much as I do myself. But have no fear, for I shall keep him so well under control that you will be perfectly safe." They answered: "That will be fine!" Then they entered the castle and went on until they met knights and ladies and pleasant damsels, who greeted him and helped him to dismount and remove his armor, and they said to him: "Welcome, fair Lord, among us, and God grant you stay here until you may leave with great joy and great honor!"

From the highest to the lowest they strove to give him a joyous welcome, and with great joy they led him to the castle. But when they had welcomed him so joyfully a sorrow caused them to forget their joy; and they began to cry out, and weep, and scratch their faces. Thus they went on at great length, being joyful and then weeping: they were joyful in order to honor their guest, but their hearts were not really in it, for they were dismayed because of an evil adventure that they expected for the following day, and they were quite sure and certain they would have it, before noon.

My Lord Ywain was amazed that they so often changed back and forth between sorrow and joy, and he questioned the lord of the castle: "In God's name," said he, "fair dear good Sir, would it please you to explain why you have so honored me and shown so much joy and so much weeping?" "Yes, if it pleases you; but you should instead by far prefer that I keep silent and conceal our reasons. I shall never, by my will, tell you a thing that will bring you sorrow. Let us express our sorrow, and do not take it to heart."

"I could not, at any price, see you showing such grief without taking it to heart myself; rather, I very much wish to know the truth, whatever sorrow I may have on that account." "Then I shall tell you," said the lord. "A giant has done me great harm: he wanted me to give him my daughter, who surpasses in beauty all the maidens in the world. The evil giant (may God confound him!) is called Harpin of the Mountain. Never is there a day when he

64

doesn't take from me everything he can get. No one must have more cause to complain than I, or to sorrow and grieve. I should go mad from grief, for I had six knighted sons, the fairest in the world, to my mind; and the giant has taken all six of them. Right before my eyes he killed two, and tomorrow he will kill the other four, unless I find someone who dares to battle with him, to save my sons, or unless I want to surrender my daughter to him; and when he has her, he says he will hand her over to the lowest and ugliest serving-boys he can find in his house, for their pleasure, for he will no longer deign to take her himself. I can expect this grief tomorrow, unless God comes to my assistance. And for this reason it is no wonder, dear fair Lord, that we weep; but for you, as much as we are able, we shall at the same time strive to show a joyful countenance, for he is mad who brings a valiant and honorable man into his company, if he does him no honor, and you look like a valiant man to me. Now I have told you the sum, Sir, of our great distress. The giant has left us neither castle nor fortress except for what we have in here. You saw yourself, if you paid attention this evening, that he did not leave anything worth a plank, apart from these walls, which have remained; rather, he has razed the whole town. When he had taken away what he wanted, he set fire to what was left. And so he has done me many an evil turn."

My Lord Ywain listened to everything that his host told him, and when he had listened to all, he replied with something which pleased him. "Sir," he said, "I am very vexed and greatly saddened by your troubles, but I wonder at one thing, if you have not sought help at the court of good King Arthur. No man is so valiant that he could not find at his court some who would wish to test their valor against his." And then the rich man explained and revealed that he would have been well served, if he had only known where to find my Lord Gawain. "He would not have undertaken it in vain, for my wife is his own sister, but a knight from a strange land, who

65

went to the court to ask for the King's wife, has gone away with her. Yet he never would have taken her away, for anything he could have done, had it not been for Kay, who deceived the King so that he gave him the Queen and put her in his care. He was mad and she was foolish to trust in his protection, and in turn I am the one who has too great damage and too great loss, for it is absolutely certain that my Lord Gawain, the valiant, would have come here with great speed, for the sake of his niece and his nephews, had he known about this misfortune; but he does not know of it, wherefore my grief is so great that my heart is near to bursting; instead he has gone after that knight—may God send him shame and sorrow!—who took the Queen away."

My Lord Ywain made no end of sighs when he heard this; because of the pity he felt he replied: "Fair, sweet and gentle Sir, I should gladly place myself in jeopardy and in peril, if the giant and your sons came here tomorrow at such a time that there would not be to great a delay, for I shall be elsewhere tomorrow at the hour of noon, as I have promised." "Fair Sir," said the worthy man, "I thank you a hundred times in one, for your good will." And all the people of the castle did likewise, each in turn.

Then out of a room came the maiden, who was attractive in body and fair and pleasing of face. She came very simply, dejected and silent, and there was never an end to her sorrowing: she kept her head bowed toward the ground, and her mother also came beside her, for the lord, who had sent for them, wanted them to meet his guest. Wrapped in their cloaks they came, in order to hide their tears, and he ordered them to open their cloaks, and to lift up their heads, and said: "What I order you to do must not grieve you, for a worthy man of very high lineage has been sent to us by God and good fortune, and he assures me that he will fight the giant. Now delay no more before you throw yourselves at his feet."

"May God never let me see that!" my Lord Ywain immediately replied. "Truly, it would in no way be proper for the sister or the niece of my Lord Gawain to be at my feet, at any price. God forbid that pride should extend so far in me as to let them place themselves at my feet! Truly, I would never forget the shame which I should have from that. But I should be grateful to them if they would take comfort until tomorrow, when they may see whether God wishes to help them. You need ask no more of me, provided the giant comes early enough so that I am not forced to break my promise elsewhere, for I would not let anything keep me from being present for the most important matter, in truth, that I may ever have."

So he did not want to reassure them completely, for he feared that the giant would not come early enough so that he could return in time to the maiden who was imprisoned in the chapel. And yet he did promise them enough to put them in a hopeful frame of mind. They thanked him one and all, for they placed much trust in his prowess, and thought that he must surely be a worthy and valiant man because of the company of the lion, who lay down beside him as gently as a lamb would have done. Because of the hopes they had in him they took comfort and were joyful, and never showed any more grief. When it was time, they showed him to a brightly lit room where he was to sleep, and the damsel and her mother both attended him when he went to bed, for they already esteemed him very highly, and they would have done so a hundred thousand times more if they had been aware of his courtesy and his great prowess. He and the lion lay together in that room and rested, but other people dared not lie there; rather they closed the door so well upon them that they could not get out again before dawn of the following day.

When the room was opened up again, Ywain rose and heard mass and waited, because of the promise he had made them, until the hour of prime [about 6:00 a.m.]. He then called to the lord of the castle himself, and said to him, so that all could hear: "Sire, I can wait no longer, but rather

I shall leave, may it not grieve you, for it is not possible for me to stay here any longer. But know full well that willingly and gladly, if I had not had such urgent business and were it not so far away, I should have stayed a while longer for the sake of the nephews and the niece of my Lord Gawain whom I so dearly love."

Then all the maiden's blood quivered and started, from fear, and so did the lady's and the lord's; they were so afraid that he would leave that they all, from their standing position, wanted to throw themselves at his feet, but then they remembered that such an action would be displeasing to him. Then the lord offered to give him some of his wealth, if he would take anything, whether land or other goods, if only he would wait a bit longer. And Ywain answered: "God forbid that I ever have any of it!" And the maiden, who was very much afraid, began to weep bitterly, and she begged him to stay. Like one distraught and full of anguish she begged him, in the name of the glorious Queen of Heaven and the angels, and in the name of God, not to leave, but rather to stay a little longer, and also in the name of her uncle, whom he said he knew and loved and esteemed.

Then Ywain was overcome by a great pity when he heard her invoke the name of the man he loved most and also the Queen of the Heavens, and God himself, who is the honey and the sweetness of mercy. He heaved a sigh of anguish, for not for the kingdom of Tarsus would he wish that she to whom he had promised assistance be burned at the stake. His life would not last long, or else he would lose his mind, if he could not get there in time; and, on the other hand, in great distress, the great nobility of his friend my Lord Gawain held him back, so that his heart nearly split in two, when he could no longer stay.

Nevertheless he still did not leave, but rather stayed and waited until the giant came galloping along, leading the knights; by his neck he held a stake, large and square, sharpened at one end, with which he frequently prodded them. And they did not have on a single piece of clothing worth a straw, except for dirty and filthy shirts; their hands and feet were bound with ropes, and they sat on four limping pack-horses, all thin and weak and broken-down. They came riding along a wood, and a dwarf, like a swollen toad, had tied them tail-to-tail, and he rode beside all four of them. He never left off striking them with a four-knotted whip, and so thought that he was acting very nobly; he struck them so much that they were bleeding. Thus the giant and the dwarf together basely brought them along.

The giant stopped before the door, in the middle of a flat space, and called out to the lord that he challenged his sons to mortal combat, if he did not deliver his daughter to him, and that he would turn her over to his pack of scullions, as their prostitute, for he did not love nor value her so much as to deign to debase himself by taking her. She would have with her at all times a thousand scullions, lousy and naked like beggars and slovens, and all would make their contribution. The good man nearly went mad when he heard the giant say that he would put his daughter into prostitution, or else that his four sons would forthwith be killed, before his very eyes; he was as distressed as a person who would rather be dead than alive. He repeatedly called himself wretched and miserable, and wept bitterly and sighed.

Then my Lord Ywain, the noble and gentle, began to say to him, "Sire, this giant who is boasting outside is very wicked and bold, but may God never permit him to have any power over your daughter! He greatly despises and debases her. It would be too great a misfortune if a creature so beautiful and born of such high lineage was abandoned to scullions. Bring me my arms and my horse! And have the drawbridge lowered, and let me cross it! One of us will have to be defeated, either I or he, I know not which. If I could humiliate the evil wretch who continues to mistreat us here, so that he would free your sons, and come before you to make amends for the shameful things he has said to you, then I should like to commend you to God, and go on to my other business." Then they brought out his horse and gave him all his armor; they worked hard at arming him, and quickly and well they prepared him; they took as little time as they could in arming him.

When they had equipped him properly, there was nothing left but to lower the bridge and to let him go. They lowered it for him, and he went forth, but the lion in no way stayed behind. And those who did stay behind commended him to God, for they were very much afraid that the demon, the malevolent one, who had killed many a valiant man before their eyes, on the spot, would do the same to him. And they prayed God to protect him from death, and to bring him back alive and well, and let him kill the giant. Each prayed God fervently, according to what he desired.

And the giant came toward Ywain very fiercely, and threatened him, and said: "Whoever sent you here didn't love you much, by my eyes! Surely, he couldn't have done any better to take revenge against you, in any way. He has done a good job of taking revenge for whatever wrong you did him." "You've started a quarrel for nothing!" said Ywain, who feared him not at all; "now do your best, and I'll do mine, for useless words are tedious to me." Then without delay my Lord Ywain attacked him, for he was eager to be on his way; he went to strike him in the chest, which was protected by a bearskin. And the giant came running at him from the other side, with his stake. My Lord Ywain gave him such a blow in the chest that he pierced the skin; he dipped the iron point of his lance in the blood of the giant's body, as in a sauce; and the giant struck him with his club so hard that he made him fold over. My Lord Ywain drew his sword, with which he knew how to deal great blows. He found the giant without protection, for he so trusted in his strength that he did not deign to arm himself; and he who held his sword drawn made an attack upon him. With the cutting edge, not with the flat, he struck him so that he carved a slice from his cheek. And the giant, in turn, gave Ywain such a blow that he brought his head down all the way to the neck of his charger.

At that blow the lion's hair stood on end, and he made ready to help his master, and he leaped in anger, and with great strength he seized hold, and split like bark the giant's hairy bearskin; underneath he took away a large piece of his haunch, slicing through the nerves and muscles. And the giant tore away from him, and bellowed and cried like a bull, for the lion had severely wounded him. He raised his club with both hands and tried to strike, but he missed, and the lion jumped back, and the blow was lost and fell harmlessly beside my Lord Ywain so that it touched neither one of them. And my Lord Ywain raised his arm and struck two blows. Before the giant had taken heed, Ywain, with the edge of his sword, had severed his shoulder from his torso. With the other blow, under the breast, he thrust the whole blade of his sword through the giant's liver. The giant fell; death was upon him, and if a giant oak fell I do not believe it would make a greater crash than did the giant as he fell. All those who were on the battlements were very glad to see that blow.

Then it could be seen who was the fastest, for all ran toward the spoils, just like dogs that have hunted the beast until they have caught it. So they all ran, men and women, without dissimulation, each trying to be the first to reach the place where the giant lay on his back. The lord himself ran there, as did the daughter, the mother, and all the people of the court. Now the four brothers were joyful, for they had suffered much harm. They were quite sure that they could not detain my Lord Ywain, no matter what might happen, so they begged him to come back to stay and take his pleasure as soon as he had finished his business where he was going.

And he replied that he dared not promise them anything, for he could in no way guess whether it would turn out well or ill for him; but to the lord he said this much, that he wanted his four sons and his daughter to take the dwarf, and go to my Lord Gawain, once they knew that he had returned, and they should recount how he had conducted himself, for he who does not want his good acts known does them for naught. And they replied: "This good act will never be kept secret, for that would not be right. We will gladly do whatever you wish—but we wish to ask you this, Sire: when we come before him, whom can we praise, if we do not know how to name you?" And he answered: "You can tell him this much, when you come before him, that I told you my name was the Knight of the Lion. And with this I must ask you to tell him on my behalf that he knows me well, and I him, and yet he does not know who I am. I ask you nothing more. Now I must leave here, and that is what most troubles me, that I may have stayed here too long; for before noon has come and gone, I shall have much to do elsewhere, if I can get there in time."

Then he left, to stay there no more. But first the lord begged him, as persuasively as he could, to take his four sons with him. There was not one of them who would not strive to serve him, if he so directed; but it did not please him that anyone should accompany him: he rode away alone and left them. And as soon as he was on his way, he headed back toward the chapel at full speed. The way was both fine and straight, and he had no trouble following it. But before he could come to the chapel, the maiden was taken from it, and the pyre made ready, where she was to be put. Those who wrongly charged her with what she never thought of doing had bound her and were leading her to the stake, dressed in nothing but her shift.

My Lord Ywain came to the fire wherein they wanted to throw her, and all this must have grieved him deeply; anyone who doubted it in the least would be neither courteous nor wise. It is true that it distressed him greatly, but he was confident that God and right would be on his side and would help him: he trusted very much in these companions, and he had no hatred for his lion, either. At full gallop he rode into the press, crying: "Release the maiden, evil people! It is not right that she should be put in any pyre or fire, for she has done nothing to deserve it." And the people moved apart on each side, and made way for him, and he was very eager to see with his eyes her whom his heart saw wherever she might be; he sought her with his eyes until he found her, and he put his heart to such a test that he had to curb and restrain it as one restrains with great difficulty, with a strong bridle, a pulling horse. And yet he looked upon her gladly, sighing, but his sighs were never so free that anyone could notice them; rather, he held them back with great anguish.

And he was overcome with pity, for he saw and heard the poor women who were bitterly grieving and saying: "Oh, God, how you have forgotten us, for now we shall be lost because we are losing such a fine friend, and such a source of counsel and aid, as she was for us at court! On her advice my lady clothed us in her miniver-trimmed dresses. Now things will be very different for us, for there will no longer be anyone to speak in our behalf. May God curse those who take her away from us! Evil be to those through whom we lose her, for we shall suffer greatly because of this. There will no longer be anyone to say or advise: 'This miniver cloak and this overgarment and this dress, dear Lady, give to this noble woman, for truly, if you send it to her, it will be well employed, for she has great need of it.' Never will a word be said of this, for no longer is anyone noble or courteous; rather, each one asks for himself, and not for any other unless there be some need to do so."

Thus they lamented, and my Lord Ywain was in their midst, and clearly heard their complaints, which were neither false nor feigned. And he saw Lunete on her knees, undressed but for her shift; she had already been confessed, and had admitted her sins and asked God forgiveness for them. And he who had loved her well came toward her, and raised her up and said: "Maiden, where are those who blame and accuse you? If they do not refuse it, I shall immediately offer them battle." And she who had not yet seen him said to him: "Sire, in God's name, come to my great need! Those who bear false witness are all prepared against me, here; if you had delayed a little more I should soon have been ashes and cinders. You have come to defend me, and may God grant you the power to do so, just as surely as I am innocent of the blame of which I am accused."

The seneschal and his brothers heard these words: "Ha!" said they, "woman, miserly creature when telling the truth, and generous in lying! Anyone who takes on such a great burden because of what you say is very unwise; he is a very unfortunate knight who has come here to die for you, for he is alone and there are three of us. But I advise him to go back, before it turns out the worse for him." And he replied, very angry: "Whoever is afraid, let him flee! I am not so afraid of your three shields that I will go away vanquished without a blow. Then I should certainly act unchivalrously, if I, quite healthy, safe and sound, left you the field of battle! Never, while I am alive and well, will I flee because of such threats. But I advise you to have the maiden declared innocent, whom you have so wrongfully accused, for she says, and I believe her, and she has sworn to me, upon peril of her soul, that she never committed, nor spoke, nor thought any treason against her lady. I fully believe all she has told me of this; and I shall defend her, if I can, for I find her right on my side. And the truth of the matter is that God is also on the side of right, and God and right are together; and when they come to my side, then I have better company than you do, and better help."

And the other answered very foolishly that he could put to use against him whatever he liked, provided that the lion not harm them. And Ywain said that he never brought his lion there for a champion, nor did he wish to involve any but himself in the fight, but if his lion attacks him, he should defend himself against him, for he can make no guarantee. The seneschal answered: "Whatever you say, if you don't control your lion and make him stay put, then you have no reason to stay here; but go away again, and you'll act wisely, for throughout this land people know how she betrayed her lady; it is right that the punishment for that be given in fire and flame." "May it not please the Holy Spirit," said he who well knew the truth; "may God not let me move from here until I have delivered her." Then he told the lion to withdraw, and to lie still; and he did as his master ordered.

The lion withdrew. Then the speaking and the quarreling ceased between them, and they took their distance; the three came charging toward him together, and he came toward them at a walk, for he did not want to let himself go nor to get worked up at the very first blows. He let them splinter their lances and kept his own intact; he offered them his shield as a target and broke the lance of each. Then he galloped off until he had put an acre of ground between himself and them; but he came quickly back to the business at hand, for he did not want to stay long. When he came back Ywain reached the seneschal before his two brothers: he broke his lance on his body, so that he carried him to the ground, despite his wishes; he gave him such a good blow that he lay stretched out for a long time so that he could do no more harm. Then the other two came at Ywain: with their naked swords they both gave him great blows, but they received greater ones from him, for a single one of his blows was exactly worth two of theirs. He defended himself so well against them that they could gain no advantage over him, until the seneschal got back up and attacked him with all his strength; then the others strove with him until they wore him down and overcame him. And the lion, who was watching this, waited no more to assist his master, for his help was needed, it seemed to him; and all the ladies together, who dearly loved the damsel, called very often upon the Lord God, and fervently prayed that he would at no price allow the death or the defeat of the knight who had risked himself for her. The ladies helped him with their prayers, for they had no other weapons. And the lion helped him so that at the first attack he struck the seneschal, who was on foot, with such rage that he made the links of mail fly from his hauberk as if they had been straws, and pulled him down so strongly that he tore the flesh from his shoulder and his side. Whatever he reached he tore away so that his entrails appeared. The other two paid for this blow.

Now the two sides were even on the field. The seneschal could not escape death: he was wallowing and rolling around in the crimson wave of the blood that was gushing from his body. The lion attacked the others, for my Lord Ywain could not drive him back, neither with blows nor with threats, though he tried hard to do so; but the lion surely knew that his master did not detest his aid, but rather loved him the more for it; so he attacked them ferociously until they suffered from his blows and injured and maimed him in turn. When my Lord Ywain saw his lion wounded, his heart was very angry within his chest, and he was not wrong; he strove mightily to wreak vengeance, he went at them so savagely and made it so hard for them that they gave up defending themselves against him and placed themselves at his mercy because of the aid given him by the lion, who was now sorely afflicted, because he was wounded in two places, and was quite rightly distraught. And for his part my Lord Ywain was not completely unscathed, but rather was wounded in many places; but he was far less upset by this than by the suffering of his lion.

Now had he rescued his damsel, just as he had wished, and the lady quite willingly pardoned her and renounced her anger. And they who had set up the pyre to burn her were burned in it instead, for it is a principle of justice that he who wrongly condemns another must die by that same death to which he had condemned the other. Now Lunete was joyous and gay when she was reconciled with her lady, and they

76

were so joyful that no people ever displayed such great joy, and all offered their service to their lord, just as they should have done, but without recognizing him; even the lady who had his heart, and did not know it, begged him to stay until he had recovered, and his lion as well. And he said: "Lady, it will not be today that I stay in this place, until my lady pardons me and renounces her anger and her wrath. Then my torments will all be over." "Surely," said she, "this grieves me, and I do not consider very courteous the lady who bears you ill will. She should not forbid access to her door to a knight of your value, unless he had committed too great a fault against her." "Lady," said he, "though it be painful to me, everything that suits her pleases me, but do not question me on his subject, for I would not for any thing reveal my wrong and my misdeed, except to those who know them well." "Then does someone know it, apart from you two?" "Yes, truly, my Lady." "And tell us your name, fair Lord, if you please, and then you will leave and all will be even between us." "Even, my Lady? It would not be so; I owe you more than I could repay; nevertheless, I must not conceal from you how I have people call me: never will you hear anyone speak of the Knight of the Lion who is not speaking of me: that is the name by which I wish to be called." "In God's name, fair Lord, how is it that we never saw you nor ever heard your name?" "Lady, in this way you may know that I am not very well known." Then the lady repeated: "Again, if it were not disagreeable to you, I would ask you to remain." "Certainly, Lady, I would not do so until I knew for certain that I had my lady's good will." "Then may God be with you, fair Lord, and may it please him to turn your sorrow and your grief to joy!" "Lady," said he, "may God hear you!" Then he said softly, between his teeth: "Lady, you bear the key, and you have the lock and the chest where my joy is, but you know it not."

Then he left, full of anguish, and there was no one who recognized him, except for Lunete, who accompanied him for a long way. Lunete alone accompanied him, and he repeatedly begged her that never through her should be revealed what champion she had had. "Sire," said she, "it will not be." After that he also begged her to remember him to intercede in his favor with his lady, if she had the occasion to do so. And she said that he should say no more on the subject, for she would never be forgetful or cowardly or lazy on that account, and he thanked her a hundred times.

He went off, pensive and troubled because of his lion, whom he had to carry, since he was not able to follow. With moss and ferns he made a litter for him on his shield; when he had made his bed for him he laid him on it as gently as he could, and carried him stretched out within the hollow of his shield. So he carried him within his shield until he came before the door of a very strong and beautiful castle; he found it closed, and so he called, and the door-keeper opened it so quickly that he could not call a second word after the first. He put his hand on the reins, and said: "Fair Sir, I present to you as a gift my lord's house, if it pleases you to stay there." "That gift," said he, "I willingly accept, for I have great need of it and it is time to seek shelter." Then he passed through the door and saw the household all massed together, all coming to meet him. They greeted him and helped him dismount; some took the shield with the lion and placed it on a stone, and others took his horse and put it in a stable; the squires, as they ought to do, took his arms and received them. When the lord of the house heard the news he came immediately to the courtyard, and greeted him, and the lady came after him, and his sons and all his daughters; there were great quantities of other people, and they gave him lodging with great joy; they put him in a peaceful room because they found he was ill, and similarly they took good care to put his lion with him; and two maidens who knew much of medicine took care of curing him, and they were daughters of the lord of that place. I do not know how many days he stayed there, until he and his lion were cured and they had to leave again.

But during that time it happened that the lord of the Black

Thorn had quarreled with Death, and Death attacked him so violently that he was forced to die. After his death it happened that the elder of his two daughters said that she would freely have all the land for as long as she lived, and that her sister would never have any share of it. And the younger sister said that she would go to the court of King Arthur to seek assistance in defending her land. And when the other saw that her sister was quite unwilling to give up all the land without a fight, she was very worried, and said that, if she could, she would arrive at the court first. She quickly made ready and prepared herself, and she neither tarried nor paused, but rather traveled until she came to the court; and the younger sister came along after her and hastened as much as she could, but she wasted her time and her efforts, for the elder sister had already pleaded her case before my Lord Gawain, and he had granted her all that she had requested of him. But there was such an agreement between them that if anyone learned of it from her, he would never arm himself in her behalf; and she agreed to this.

Then the other sister came to court, dressed in a short cloak of rich cloth trimmed with ermine: it was the third day since the Queen had come back from the prison where Méléagant had kept her with all the other prisoners; only Lancelot had remained inside the tower, a victim of Méléagant's treachery. And on that very same day that the maiden came to the court the news had arrived of the cruel and wicked giant whom the Knight of the Lion had killed in battle. The nephews of my Lord Gawain had greeted him on his behalf. His niece had told him in detail of the great service that he had rendered them out of love for him, and she said that he knew him well, yet knew not who he was.

She who was very troubled and worried and frightened heard this; she thought to find no help or assistance at court, since the best knight failed her, for she had tried in many ways, appealing to love and resorting to prayers, to win my Lord Gawain to her cause, and he had said to her: "Friend, in vain you beg me, for I cannot do it, since I have undertaken another matter which I would not abandon." And the maiden immediately left him and went before the King. "King," said she, "I came to you and to your court to seek help; I find none, and I am amazed that I can find no help there. But I should act improperly if I went away without permission. And I wish my sister to know, however, that I would share my wealth with her on a basis of love and friendship, if she were willing to do so, but never will I abandon my inheritance to her under threat of force, if I can help it, as long as I can find help or assistance." "You speak sensibly," said the King, "and while she is here I advise her and request that she let you have what is rightfully yours." And she who was sure of the help of the world's best knight answered: "Sire, may God confound me if ever I cede her either castle, or town, or clearing, or wood, or plain, or anything else from my land. But if some knight dares take up arms for her, let him, whoever he may be, who is willing to defend her right, come forth immediately." "You do not make a proper offer," said the King, "for more time is necessary; if she wishes she may have up to forty days to seek a champion; all courts agree to this." And she said: "My fair Sire and King, you can establish your laws as you please and as seems good to you; it is not fitting or proper for me to contradict or oppose you; I must therefore accept the delay, if she requests it." And the younger sister said that she did request and desire it. Then she commended the King to God and left the court, thinking that in all her life she would never stop seeking, in all lands, the Knight of the Lion, who puts his efforts in the service of ladies and maidens in need of help.

So she began her quest and passed through many lands without ever hearing any news of him, which caused her such grief that she fell ill. But fortunately it happened that she came to the home of a friend who was very fond of her. It was obvious from her face that she was not at all well. They strove to keep her there until she told them of her business;

then another maiden took up the journey which she had begun: she took up the quest in her place. So the younger daughter stayed there.

And the other maiden traveled all day long, all alone and at top speed, until it grew dark. The darkness troubled her greatly, and her troubles were doubled by the fact that it was raining as violently as God could make it rain, and she was deep in the woods. And although the night and the woods troubled her greatly, the rain troubled her even more than the night or the woods. And the road was so bad that her horse was often almost up to the cinches in mud; and well might she be very much afraid, a maiden in the woods, without escort, in bad weather, in the dark of night, so dark that she could not see the horse upon which she was sitting. And for this reason she constantly called first upon God, and then upon His Mother, and then all the saints; and through the night she said many prayers that God might lead her to a place of lodging and get her out of that wood.

She prayed so much that at length she heard a horn, which made her very happy, for she believed she would find a place of lodging, provided she could reach it; she headed in the direction of the sound until she came upon a road, and the road led her straight toward the horn whose sound she heard, for it sounded three times, very long and loudly; and she went straight to the sound, until she came to a cross to the right of the road; there she thought that the horn and he who had blown it might be found; she spurred in that direction until she drew near to a bridge, and saw the white walls and the barbican of a small round castle. So by chance she arrived at the castle, and was guided to it, by means of the voice which led her there. It was the voice of the horn, sounded by a guard mounted on the walls, that had drawn her there. As soon as the guard saw her, he greeted her and then came down from the wall, and took the key to the door, opened it, and said: "Welcome, maiden, whoever you may be. You will have good lodging tonight." "I ask nothing else for tonight," the maiden answered; and he led her in. After the travail and the difficulty she had had that day, she was fortunate to reach that place of lodging, for she was well taken care of there.

After supper her host questioned her, and asked her where she was going and what she was seeking. And she answered: "I seek someone I never saw, to my knowledge, nor ever met, but he has a lion with him and I've been told that, if I find him, I can have great faith in him." Said he, "For my part, I can testify to that, for in my very great need God brought him to me a few days ago. Blessed be the paths by which he came to my dwelling, for he avenged me against a mortal enemy of mine, which gave me great joy, for he slew him right before my eyes. Tomorrow, outside that door, you can see the body of a great giant whom he killed so quickly that he scarcely worked up a sweat at it." "For God's sake, Sire," said the maiden, "do tell me truly if you know which way he went from here and if he stayed in any place." "I cannot, though God see me! But tomorrow I can certainly put you on the road he took when he left." "And may God," said she, "lead me there where I may learn of him, for if I find him I shall be very glad."

Thus they spoke at great length, until at last they went to bed. The maiden was up at the crack of dawn, for she was extremely anxious to find what she was looking for. And the lord of the house got up, and all his companions; and they set her on the road that led straight to the spring under the pine. And she strove to go directly toward the castle; when she got there she asked the first people she met if they could tell her where to find the lion and the knight who had accompanied one another. And they told her that they had seen them conquer three knights right there on that piece of ground. And she immediately said: "For God's sake, since you have told me this much, do not hide from me anything else you can tell." But they said, "No, we know no more beyond what we have told you; we do not know what became of him. If she for whom he came here does not tell you further news of him, then no one can, and, if you wish to speak to her, you need go no further, for she has gone into that church to hear mass and to pray to God, and she has stayed there so long that she has no doubt finished by now."

While they were speaking thus Lunete came out of the church; and they said to her: "There she is." And the maiden went to meet her. As soon as they had greeted one another, the maiden asked for the news she was seeking; and Lunete said that she would have one of her palfreys saddled, for she would go with her, and would lead her to an enclosure where she had accompanied him. And the maiden thanked her with all her heart. The palfrey was not long in coming; they brought it and she mounted. As they rode Lunete told her how she had been accused and charged with treason and how the pyre had been lit where she was to be put, and how he came to help her when her need was greatest. So speaking she accompanied her until she brought her to the straight road where my Lord Ywain had left her. When she had accompanied her that far, she said to her: "You will keep to this road until you come to some place where, if it please God and the Holy Spirit, you will have more reliable news of him than I can tell. I remember well that I left him quite near here, or at this very spot; we saw each other no more after that, nor do I know what he has done since, for he was in great need of balm or plaster for his wounds when he took leave of me. I send you after him in this direction, and God grant that you find him well, if it please Him, and today rather than tomorrow. Now go; I commend you to God, for I dare not follow you further, for fear that my lady would become angry with me."

Then they parted: one turned back, and the other went on until she found the castle where my Lord Ywain had stayed until he was completely well again. And she saw people before the door, ladies, knights, and men-at-arms, and the lord of the house; she greeted them and questioned them: if they knew, let them tell her news, and let them inform her of a knight she was seeking. "He is such that he will never be without a lion, or so I have heard." "Upon my word, maiden," said the lord, "he just left us; you will still catch up with him today, if you know how to follow his tracks, but do not tarry too long." "Sire," said she, "God forbid! But tell me now in what direction I should follow him." And they told her: "Straight on this way," and they asked her to greet him on their behalf. But it availed them little, for she paid no heed to their request, but instead set off at full gallop, for ambling seemed to her too slow, and yet her palfrey ambled at great speed. So she galloped through the mud, just as where the road was smooth and flat, until she saw the knight who was accompanied by the lion. Then she was overjoyed, and said: "God, help! Now I see what I have so long pursued; I have followed and tracked him very well. But if I pursue and overtake him, what good will it do me, if I do not catch him? Little or none, and that's the truth; if he does not come along with me, then I have wasted my efforts." So speaking she hastened on, her palfrey all in a sweat; she stopped, and greeted him, and he at once replied to her: "God save you, fair maiden, and deliver you from care and sorrow!" "And you, Sire, in whom I have hope, for you could indeed take me from them!" Then she placed herself beside him and said: "Sire, I have sought you. The great fame of your merit has made me grow very tired in pursuit of you, and pass through many lands. I have sought you so long—God be thanked!—that I have caught up with you here, and if I have endured some pain in doing so, I do not grieve at all for that, nor do I complain, nor even remember it; my members are all made lighter, for suffering was removed from me as soon as I caught up with you. But it is not my own need; I am sent to you by someone better than myself, a more noble and more worthy woman, but if she has erred on your account, then your fame has betrayed her, for she expects no help nor aid except from you; the damsel, whom her sister wishes to disinherit, seeks no one else to get involved in defending her interests; nor can anyone convince her that anyone else could help her in this matter. And know in all truth that if you can win the prize in this, you will have conquered and regained the honor of the disinherited sister, and increased your own prestige. She herself sought you to defend her inheritance, because of the good she hoped to gain from it, and none other would have come looking for you, but a grave illness held her back so that she was forced to stay in bed. Now answer me, if you please: will you dare come to her rescue, or will you refuse?" "I do not care for ease," said he, "for no man can make himself worthy of praise in that way, and I shall spend no time at rest, but rather will willingly follow you, my sweet friend, wherever it may please you; and if she for whom you seek me has great need of me, never fear that I shall not do all in my power to help her; now may God grant me courage and grace that I may, with his blessing, defend her rightful cause."

Thus the two of them spoke together as they rode along, until they approached the castle of Pesme-Aventure. They had no desire to go further, for the day was waning. As they were drawing near this castle all the people who saw them coming said to the knight: "Ill come, Sir, ill come! This lodging was shown you so that you would suffer evil and shame; an abbot could swear to it." "Ha!" said he, "mad and nasty people, people full of all kinds of wickedness and who have missed out on all good qualities, why have you attacked me thus?" "Why? You will know only too well if you go a bit farther! But you'll never know anything about it until you have been inside that tall fortress." My Lord Ywain then headed toward the tower, and all the people loudly shouted to him, saying: "Hoo! Hoo! Wretched man, where are you going? If ever in your life you found anyone who would cause you injury or shame, you will get so much of it where you're going that you'll never be able to tell of it." "People without honor, and without goodness," replied my Lord Ywain, "bothersome and insolent people, why do you assail me? Why do you attack me? What do you ask of me? What do you want, growling at me in this way?" "Friend, do not be angry," said a middle-aged lady who was very courteous and wise, "for surely it is not for ill that they say anything to you, but rather they are advising you, if you but knew how to understand, against taking lodging up there; they dare not tell you the reason for it, but they scold and discourage you because they want to dismay you; and they do likewise to all who come along, as a matter of custom, so that they won't go in there. And the custom is such that we dare not give lodging, whatever may happen, to any knight who comes from outside. Now the rest is up to you: no one is barring your way. If you wish, you will go up there, but if you take my advice, you'll turn back." "Lady," said he, "if I took your advice, I believe that I would have honor and advantage in so doing; but I would not know where I might still find lodging today." "Faith," said she, "I shall say no more, for that is no business of mine. Go wherever you wish. And yet I would have great joy if I saw you come back from there without too great shame; but that cannot be." "Lady," said he, "may God reward you! But my mad heart draws me there: I shall do what my heart wishes." Then he advanced toward the door, with his lion and the maiden; and the door-keeper called to him, and said: "Come quickly, come, for you have come to a place where you will be securely detained, and you are ill-come there."

So the door-keeper provoked him and urged him to come up, but it was a very ungracious invitation. And my Lord Ywain, without reply, went right on by him, and found a large hall, high and new; before it there was a yard enclosed by sharp stakes, round and thick; and between the stakes he saw inside as many as three hundred maidens, all sewing at various types of things, with golden and silken thread, each as well as she knew how. But there was such poverty there that many of them were poorly clad and did not even have belts to wear; and their tunics were torn on their breasts and their sides, and their shirts were dirty on their backs; their necks were gaunt and their faces pale from hunger and misfortune. He saw them, and they saw him, and they all lowered their heads and wept; and they remained a long time unable to do anything, nor could they raise their eyes from the ground, so down-hearted were they. When my Lord Ywain had watched them for a while, he turned around and went straight back toward the door; and the door-keeper jumped in front of him, and cried out: "It's no use, for you won't leave now, fair master; you'd like to be outside there now, but, by my head, that does you no good, for first you'll suffer so much shame that you could have no more. It was pure folly to come in here, for there's no possibility of going out again." "Nor do I seek to do so," said he, "fair brother. But tell me, upon your father's soul, where did they come from, the maidens whom I saw inside this castle weaving sheets of silk and gold embroidery? Their work pleases me greatly, but I am greatly displeased that they are so thin of body and pale of face and that they suffer so. I believe they would be very beautiful and charming, if they had what they need." "I," said he, "will tell you nothing at all; find someone else to tell you." "So I shall, since I cannot do otherwise." Then he sought until he found the door to the yard where the maidens were working; and he came before them, and greeted them all together; and he saw the teardrops run from their eyes and fall, as they wept. And he said to them: "May it please God to remove this sorrow, whose source I know not, from your hearts, and turn it into joy." One of them answered: "May God hear you in this, since you have appealed to Him! We shall not conceal from you who we are and from what land, since perhaps that is what you wish to learn." "For nothing else," said he, "did I come here."

"Sir, it happened very long ago that the King of the Isle of Maidens set out to travel to various courts and lands, in search of new things. He kept on going, like one both simple and naïve, until he fell into this trap. By great misfortune came he to this place, for we, the prisoners who are here, have the shame and evil of it, we who never deserved it. And know that you yourself can expect very great shame here, if they are unwilling to accept your offer of ransom. But in any case it so happened that my lord came to this castle where there are two sons of a devil—and don't think this is any fable, for they were born of woman and demon. And those two were to fight with the King, whose terror was exceedingly great, for he was not yet eighteen years old. They could quickly have split him in two just like a tender young lamb; and the King, who was greatly afraid, freed himself from that situation as best he could: he swore that each year, for as long as he lived, he would send here thirty of his maidens; and for this price he was allowed to go free. And it was established by oath that this tribute was to last as long as the two devils lasted; and on the day when they would be defeated and vanquished in battle, he would be freed from that obligation, and we would be delivered, we who are condemned to shame, and to pain, and to suffering; never shall we have any pleasure. But now I'm speaking very childishly, when I speak of deliverance, for never will we go forth from here; we will always weave silken cloth, and be no better clad thereby; we will always be poor and naked, and we will always be hungry and thirsty; never will we be able to earn enough to be any better fed. We have only a very scanty supply of bread: not much in the morning, and less in the evening, for from the work of our hands each of us will never have any more than four deniers out of each pound,[1] to live on; and from this we cannot have enough food and clothing, for she who earns twenty sous in a week is in no way at the end of her troubles. And know you full well that there is not one of us who does not earn twenty sous or more. A duke would be rich on that! And here we are in

---

[1] The pound (*livre*) was divided into twenty sous, each of which was further divided into twelve deniers. The maidens were thus each allowed to keep only four deniers out of every pound actually earned —one-sixtieth of their real earnings—the rest going to the exploiters of the operation.

poverty, and he for whom we toil is rich from our earnings. We stay up a large part of the night and every day we work to earn our bread, for he threatens to maim us when we rest, and so we dare not rest. But what's the use of telling you any more? We suffer so much shame and harm that I cannot tell you the fifth part of it. And it makes us mad with rage, for many times we see young and valiant knights die fighting the two devils; they pay most dearly for their lodging, just as you will do tomorrow, for all alone, with your own hand, whether you wish it or not, you will have to fight, and lose your reputation against the two living devils."

"May God, the true heavenly King," said my Lord Ywain, "protect me from that fate, and give you back honor and joy, if that be his will! Now I must go and see the people who are inside, to learn what sort of welcome they will give me." "Then go, Sir, and may He who gives and distributes all good things protect you."

Then he went until he came into the hall; there he found no one, good or evil, who would speak to him on any subject. Ywain, the maiden and the lion went through the house until they came into an orchard; they did not discuss or talk about stabling their horses. No matter! for they were well stabled by those who thought they were getting one of them. I know not whether they thought in a reasonable way, for they still had a master in perfectly good health. The horses had oats and hay and bedding right up to their bellies. And my Lord Ywain then entered the orchard, followed by his retinue. He saw a rich man lying on a silken sheet, propped up on his elbow; before him a maiden was reading from a romance, I know not on what subject, and there was also a lady who had come to listen to the romance. She too leaned on her elbow, and was the maiden's mother, and the lord was her father; they greatly enjoyed seeing and hearing her, for they had no other children. She was no more than sixteen, and so beautiful and so full of grace that the god of Love would have devoted himself to serving her, had he seen her, and never would have made her love another than himself. To serve her he would have become a man; he would have left his divinity and would have struck his own body with the dart whose wound never heals unless a disloyal doctor works on it. It is not right that anyone should recover from it unless he discovers disloyalty therein, and whoever is cured in any other way does not love loyally. I would tell you so much about this wound that I should not reach the end of it today, if it pleased you to listen. But soon someone would be sure to object that I was only speaking of fables, for people no longer care about love and no longer love the way they used to, so that they do not even wish to hear about it.

But hear now in what way, with what show and what welcome, my Lord Ywain was lodged! All who were in the orchard jumped up to greet him, and as soon as they saw him they said: "Draw near, fair Sir! By all that God can do and say may you be called blessed, you and all that is yours!" And I know not whether they were deceiving him, but they received him with great joy and acted as though it pleased them greatly that he should be lodged very comfortably. Even the daughter of the lord served him and did him great honor, as one should do for one's good guest: she removed all his armor, and it was not the least of her attentions that with her own hands she washed his neck and his face; the father wanted all honor shown to him, and his daughter did just that; from a chest she drew out a pleated shirt, and a pair of white drawers, and needle and thread for his sleeves, and she dressed him and sewed on the arms.[2] Now may God grant that this friendly welcome and this service may not cost him too dearly! She gave him a new overgarment to put on over his shirt, and around his neck she attached a cloak; it had not a tear, but was made of fur and lined with costly cloth. So diligent was she in serving him that he was ashamed, and it

---

[2] The sleeves of fine shirts were made separately; they were sown on each time someone was going to wear the shirt, so that they would be of the proper length.

weighed on him, but the maiden was so courteous, and so noble and of such good family, that she still felt she was not doing enough. And she knew well that it pleased her mother that she should leave undone nothing that she felt could flatter him. That night at dinner he was served so many dishes that there were far more than enough; the service was enough to tire the servants who brought them to the table. They showed him all honor, and gave him a very comfortable bed; all withdrew and came near him no more, once he was in bed. And the lion lay at his feet, just as he was accustomed to do.

In the morning, when God, who arranges everything according to plan, had rekindled His light across the world, as early as He could, my Lord Ywain and his damsel arose very quickly. In a chapel they heard a mass which was very promptly said for them, in honor of the Holy Spirit.

After the mass my Lord Ywain heard some terrible news when he thought he might leave without any harm being done to him, but it could not be at all as he wished. When he said: "Sire, I am leaving, with your permission, if it please you," the lord of the house replied: "Friend, I do not yet grant it. I cannot do so, and for good reason: in this castle there is established a very cruel and diabolical custom, which I am constrained to observe. I shall have two of my men-at-arms come here; both are very big and strong, and rightly or wrongly you will have to take arms against the two of them. If you can defend yourself against them and conquer and kill both of them, my daughter wishes you to be her husband, and the domain of this castle awaits you, as well as all that belongs to it." "Sire," said Ywain, "I seek none of your land. Thus may God never give me any part of it, and may your daughter stay with you, though she is quite worthy of the Emperor of Germany, she is so beautiful and cultured." "Silence, fair guest," said the lord, "it is in vain that you excuse yourself, for you cannot escape. My castle and my daughter's hand and all my land must go to whoever can defeat on the field of battle those who will come to attack you.

The battle cannot be avoided nor be stopped in any way. But I know well that cowardice makes you refuse my daughter: in that way you think to avoid the battle completely; but be assured of this: without fail you will have to do battle. No knight who sleeps here can avoid it in any way; this is a custom and an established rule which will long continue to be observed, for my daughter will never be married until I see them dead or defeated." "So I must fight against them in any case, despite my own wishes; but I would gladly and very well have done without it, that I grant you. I shall do battle, though I regret it, since it cannot be avoided."

Then, hideous and black, the two sons of the devil came forth. Each of them had a horn-shaped club of cornel-wood, which they had covered with copper, and then bound with brass. They were armed from their shoulders down to their knees, but their heads and faces were unprotected, and their legs, which were not the least bit thin, were bare. And as they came, armed in this way, they held round shields, strong and light, to protect themselves. The lion began to tremble as soon as he saw them, for he knew well and could see that with those arms they were holding they were coming to fight with his master; and his hair and his mane all stood on end, and he trembled with boldness and with rage, and lashed the ground with his tail, for he wanted to save his master before they had a chance to kill him. And when they saw the lion, they said: "Vassal, your lion threatens us: either take him away from here, or else declare yourself defeated; for otherwise, I promise you, you'll have to put him somewhere so that he can't try to help you and hurt us; you'll have to play alone with us, because your lion would very willingly help you, if he could." "Take him away yourselves," said my Lord Ywain, since you are afraid of him, for it suits me just fine and greatly pleases me to have him hurt you, if ever he can, and it's a great pleasure to have him help me." "Faith," said they, "that can't be, for you'll not have any help in this. Do the best you can by yourself, without any help from anyone else. You have to be alone against the two of us; if the lion was with you, and he started mixing with us, you wouldn't be alone any more, for there'd be two of you against the two of us. So I'm telling you, you'll have to take your lion away from here, even though you don't like it." "Where do you want him to be?" asked Ywain. "Where do you want me to put him?" Then they showed him a little room and said, "Shut him up in there." "So be it, since you wish it so." Then he led him there and closed him in. People then went to get his armor, and they brought out his horse, and gave it to him, and he mounted.

Eager to bring him insult and shame, the two champions attacked, for they were no longer worried about the lion, now that he was closed up in the room. They gave him such blows with their clubs that his shield and helmet provided little protection, for when they struck him on the helmet they completley dented and broke it, and his shield broke apart and seemed to melt like ice; they made such holes in it that one could thrust a fist right through. Their blows were greatly to be feared. And what did he do to the two devils? Heated up by fear and shame, he defended himself with all his strength; valiantly he strove to deal great and heavy blows. They had no lack of his gifts, for he repaid their kindness doubly.

Now was the lion's heart pained and troubled, there in the room, for he remembered the great kindness that his master had shown him through his generosity. He would already have great need of his aid; he would gladly and generously repay this kindness, and would leave nothing out of the account if he could only get out there. He went looking around in all directions, but he could see no way out. He clearly heard the blows of the battle, perilous and villainous, which grieved him so greatly that he grew quite mad and outraged. He kept searching until at last he came to the threshold, which was rotten near the ground, and he scratched at it until he could squeeze it nearly as far as his haunches.

93

And my Lord Ywain was already very hard pressed and in a great sweat, and he found the two giants very strong and evil and hard. He had endured and returned many blows, as best he could, but he had not wounded them at all, for they knew too much of combat; and their shields were such that a sword could in no way nick them, no matter how cutting and sharp. For this reason my Lord Ywain could greatly fear death, but he held out until the lion had scratched his way out, under the threshold. If the villains were not to be defeated with his help, then they would never be, for they would never be at peace with the lion, as long as he knew they were alive. He grabbed one of them and threw him down, just like a sheep. Now the villains were afraid, and there was not a man in the whole place whose heart was not full of joy; and the one whom the lion had brought down would never get up again, if the other did not save him. He ran in that direction, to help him and also to save himself, for fear that the lion would attack him, once he had killed the one he had brought to earth. He was more afraid of the lion than of its master. Now that the monster had turned his back on him and exposed his unprotected neck, my Lord Ywain would be mad to let him live for long, for this was an excellent opportunity. The villain had abandoned his naked head and naked neck to him, and Ywain gave him such a blow that he cut the head from the trunk so smoothly that the monster had no notion of it. Next he speedily dismounted to take care of the other, whom the lion was holding, for he wanted to rescue him and take him away. But in vain: however much he was suffering, never would any doctor be there in time, for the lion had so wounded him in his attack, so very full of rage was he as he came, that the monster was mortally wounded. Yet Ywain pushed the lion back, and saw that he had completely pulled the shoulder from its socket. Ywain no longer needed to worry on his account, for the monster's club had fallen from his hands. And he lay almost like a dead man, for he neither stirred nor moved; but he could still

94

speak and said, as well as he could, "Fair Sir, please take away your lion, so that he won't touch me any more, for from now on you can do with me whatever you wish. And he who begs and asks for mercy must not fail to get it, if he does not find a pitiless man. I shall defend myself no more, nor will I get up from here, whatever force I may have; I place myself at your mercy." "Then state," said Ywain, "whether you admit that you are defeated and declare yourself beaten." "Sir," said he, "so it seems: I am defeated in spite of myself, and I declare myself beaten, I admit it." "Then you need fear me no more, and my lion will likewise leave you in peace."

Then with great haste all the people came and gathered around him, and both the lord and the lady showed him great joy, and embraced him, and spoke to him of their daughter, saying, "Now you will be our master, and lord over us, and our daughter will be your lady, for we will give her to you for your wife." "And I," said he, "give her back to you. Let whoever wishes her have her! I care not; I say this not out of disdain: let it not weigh upon you, if I do not take her, for I cannot, and I must not. But, if you please, deliver to me the captives that you have; the rule is, as you well know, that they must go away. free." "What you say is true," said the lord, "and I free them and give them to you, for there is no longer any impediment to doing so. But you will act wisely if you take my daughter, along with all my possessions: she is very beautiful, and full of grace, and learned; never will you have such a rich marriage, if you do not have this one." "Sir," said he, "you do not know my circumstances or my situation, nor do I dare tell them to you. But I know well that I am refusing what no one would refuse who was to turn his heart and mind to a beautiful and gracious maiden, for I should gladly receive her, if I could or if I were to receive this one or any other. I cannot, so know this in truth, and let me be, for the damsel who came here with me is waiting for me; she accompanied me here, and I in turn wish to keep her company, whatever must happen

95

to me thereby." " 'Wish,' fair Sir? And how will you? Never, if I do not command it and I decide to do it, will my door be opened for you; rather you will remain my prisoner; you show haughty pride and gravely err when I beg you to take my daughter, and you disdain her." "Disdain, Sir? I do not, by my soul, but cannot take a wife nor stay at any price. I shall follow the damsel who leads me, for it cannot be otherwise. But, if you please, with my right hand I shall promise you, and you believe me in this, that as you now see me I shall return, if ever I can, and then I shall take your daughter and do whatever pleases you." "Cursed," said he, "be anyone who asks faith or pledge or promise from you! If my daughter pleases you, you will speedily return; never for faith nor for oath, I believe, will you return sooner. Now go, for I relieve you from all pledges and all promises. If you are detained by rain or wind or by nothing at all, it won't matter to me! I shall never consider my daughter of so little worth that I should force her upon you. Now go on about your business, for it's all the same to me whether you come back or stay elsewhere."

Then my Lord Ywain departed and stayed no more in the castle, and he took away with him the liberated prisoners whom the lord had given him poor and ill appareled, but now they considered themselves rich. Out of the castle all together, before him, two by two they came, and I do not believe that they would have shown greater joy than they showed him if He who made the whole world had come down from heaven to earth. All the people who had tried their hardest to shame him now came to make peace and thank him, and went along accompanying him, but he said that he knew nothing about that: "I do not know," said he, "what you are saying, and so I declare you free from any debt to me, for you never said anything I might take ill, as far as I recall." They were very happy because of what they heard, and they praised his courtliness very highly. Then they all commended him to God, for they had accompanied him a long way; and in turn the damsels asked his permission to leave, and went away. They all bowed to him as they left, and they hoped and prayed that God might grant him joy and health and to arrive as he wished wherever he might go. And he, who was very impatient to be on his way, replied that he hoped God would save them: "Go," said he, "and may God lead you healthy and happy to your homelands." Then they set on their way, showing great joy as they went. And my Lord Ywain immediately rode off in the other direction.

He went on traveling at great speed all the days of the week, since the maiden who was leading him knew the way very well, and the castle where she had left the disinherited sister, sick and discouraged. But when she heard the news of the arrival of the maiden and the Knight of the Lion, her heart was completely full of the joy which this caused her, for now she believed that her sister might be persuaded to leave her a part of her inheritance, if it pleased her to demand it. The damsel had long lain ill, and only recently had gotten up from her illness; it had deeply tormented her, and her face showed it clearly. At their meeting she went to him right away, without delay; she greeted him, and honored him in every way she could. It is not necessary to speak of the joy that reigned that night at the castle: never a word shall be spoken of it, for there would be too much to tell; I shall omit everything until the mounting of the following day, when they left.

Then they traveled until they saw a castle where King Arthur had been staying for a fortnight or more. And the damsel who was disinheriting her sister was there, for she had stayed near the court, waiting for the arrival of her sister, who was now drawing near. But she was very unconcerned about that, because she believed no one could find any knight who could stand up to Sir Gawain in single combat. And there remained only one day of the forty, and her claim would have been upheld without contest, by right and by judgment, if that one day had gone by. But there was still much more to be done than she thought or believed.

In a low and narrow lodging-place outside the castle they lay that night, where no one knew them; for if they had slept in the castle, everyone would have recognized them, and they did not want that to happen. They came hastily out of their lodgings as soon as dawn appeared; then they hid and lay low until it was broad daylight.

I know not how many days had passed since my Lord Gawain had taken lodging elsewhere, so that no one at court had any news of him, except for the maiden for whom he wished to fight. He had gone three or four leagues away from the court, and he came to court so equipped that he could not be recognized by those who would readily have recognized him by the arms he bore. The damsel, who was quite obviously in the wrong toward her sister, in the sight of all presented him at court, for she intended to have him defend her in the quarrel in which she was in the wrong, and she said to the King: "Sire, time is passing, and it will soon be past *none* [about 3:00 P.M.], and today is the last day. Now it is clear that I am ready to defend my claim; if my sister were going to return, we should not have needed to wait so long. I can thank God that she does not now return. It really seems she can do no better, and I have gone to all this trouble for nothing; I have been ready every day, right to the last, to defend what is mine. I have defended it all without a battle, so now it is quite right that I should go enjoy my inheritance in peace, for I shall never more answer to my sister in this, as long as I live, and she will live in sorrow and misery."

And the King, who knew very well that the maiden was in the wrong and behaving disloyally towards her sister, said to her: "Friend, at a royal court one must wait, by my faith, until the King's justice has deliberated and rendered his decision. There must be no cheating, for I believe your sister will yet arrive here in time."

Before the King had finished saying this, he saw the Knight of the Lion, and the maiden beside him; the two of them came with no other company, for they had slipped away from the lion: he had remained where they had spent the night. The King saw the maiden, and did not fail to recognize her, and it pleased him greatly when he saw her, for he was on her side of the quarrel, because he understood justice. His joy at this was such that he immediately said to her: "Now, forward, beauty, God save you!" When the elder sister heard this, she gave a start, and turned around, and saw her sister and the knight whom she had brought to defend her cause, and she became blacker than earth. The younger sister was greeted by all, and she went before the King, where he was seated. When she was before him she said: "God save the King and all his company! King, if my cause can now be defended by any knight, then it shall be by this one who, in his goodness, has followed me all the way here, and this generous and noble knight would have had much to do elsewhere, but he took such pity on me that he put aside all his business for mine. Now my lady, my very dear sister, whom I love as much as my own self, would act nobly and well if she let me have so much of what is rightfully mine that there might be peace between us; I ask nothing that is rightfully hers." "Nor I, in truth," said she, "of yours: you have no right to anything, nor will you ever have; you'll never be able to preach so much that you'll get anything by preaching; you can just dry up from grief." And the younger sister, who knew very well what was fitting, and was very well-bred and courteous, promptly replied: "Truly," said she, "it grieves me that two such valiant men as these will fight because of the two of us; our quarrel is very small, but I cannot give it up, for I would lose too much thereby. And so I should be more grateful to you if you would let me have my rightful share." "Truly, whoever answered you now," said the other, "would be very foolish. May evil fire and flame burn me if I give you anything by which you'll be better off! The banks of the Danube and the Saône will sooner come together, than you'll get it without a battle." "May God, in whom I trusted and trust now, and the right I have in this, assist and keep from harm him who out of love and nobility offered himself for my service, though he does not know me, nor I him!"

After they had spoken at such length the words ceased, and they brought the knights into the middle of the court; and all the people came running, as people who want to see blows of battle, and fencing, are accustomed to do at such times. But those who wanted to do battle did not recognize each other at all—they who were accustomed to sharing great love. Then do they no longer love one another? I answer 'yes', and also 'no', and I shall prove each so that I shall find that each is correct. In truth, my Lord Gawain loves Ywain, and calls him his companion, and Ywain loves him, wherever he may be; even here, if he recognized him, he would surely receive him with open arms, and each would risk his head for the other, rather than allow him to come to harm. Is this not complete and perfect Love? Yes, surely; and is not Hate, then, in turn, quite clearly visible? Yes, for there is no doubt that each would like to break the other's head or bring him so much shame that he would be even worse off. In faith, it is a proven miracle that Love and Mortal Hate are found together. God! How can a single hostel be the dwelling-place for things that are so contrary? In a hostel, it seems to me, they cannot be together, for one could not remain with the other a single evening without there being noise and quarreling, if one knew that the other was there. But in a house there are several rooms, for it is divided into galleries and chambers, so the thing may well be thus: perhaps Love had closed himself in some hidden room, and Hate had gone to the rooms on the side by the street, wishing to be seen. Now Hate launches his attack, and spurs, and charges full force toward Love, and Love never moves. Hey! Love, where are you hiding? Come on out, and you'll see what an ally the enemies of your friends have brought into the field against you. The enemies are those same ones who love one another with a very saintly love; for love which is not false or feigned is a precious and saintly thing. So Love is completely blind, and Hate, for

100

his part, can see nothing; for Love would have to prevent them, if he recognized them, from harming one another or doing anything which might injure the other. For this reason is Love blind and defeated and deceived, for he does not recognize those who are by rights completely in his service, and yet he sees them. And Hate cannot say why one of them hates the other, yet he wants wrongly to make them fight, and each has a deadly hatred for the other. He does not love, this you may know, the man who would like to shame him, and who desires his death. What? Does Ywain then wish to kill my Lord Gawain, his friend? Yes, and Gawain him, likewise. And would my Lord Gawain like to kill Ywain with his own hands, or do worse than I have said? No indeed, I swear to you. Neither would want to have brought shame nor insult upon the other, not for all God has done for man nor for the whole Roman Empire. Now I have most shamefully lied, for it is quite obvious that each wants to attack the other, with lance in position upon its support, and each wants to injure the other, and bring him shame, and make him angry, for never will he simply pretend to do so. Now say: of whom will the vanquished complain, when one has conquered the other? For if they do indeed go against each other, I very much fear that they will keep up the battle and the melee until it is won by one side. Will Ywain be rightly able to say, if he comes out the loser, that he who did him insult or shamed him numbered him among his friends, and never called him by his name, except to call him friend and companion? Or if by chance it happens that Ywain in some way injures his friend, or somehow conquers him, will he be in the right, if he complains? No, indeed, for he will not know whom to blame.

They both took their distance, because they did not recognize one another. When they came together their heavy ash-wood lances shattered. Neither one called out to the other, for if they had done so they would have had another kind of meeting. Never then would they, upon coming together, have struck with lance or sword: they would have kissed and embraced rather than wounding one another, for indeed they were wounding and maiming one another. Their swords were not improved by this, nor their helmets, nor their shields, which were dented and split, and the edges of their swords were getting chipped and growing dull, for they exchanged such great blows—with the edges, not with the flats—and with the pommels, too, they gave such blows on their nose-pieces and on their backs, and on their brows brows and on their cheeks, which were all livid and blue where the blood was coagulating beneath; and their hauberks were so torn and their shields so cut up, that neither of them was free from wounds. and they struggled and strove so hard that breath nearly failed them; and they fought so heatedly that any jacinth or emerald that was attached to their helmets was crushed or torn away, for with the pommels they exchanged such great blows on their helmets that they were completely stunned and came close to knocking out each other's brains. Their eyes threw off sparks, for their fists were big and square, their nerves strong, their bones hard, and so they dealt terrible blows, grasping and striking heavily with their mighty swords.

When they had tired themselves for a long time, so that their helmets were broken and their hauberks all torn apart, and their shields split and broken, so much had they hammered with their swords, they drew back a bit and allowed their veins to rest and caught their breath. But they did not delay for long, but rather ran at one other more fiercely than ever, and everyone said they had never seen two more courageous knights: "They do not just play at fighting; this is serious business between them. Never will they be repaid or rewarded as they deserve." The two friends who were wounding one another heard these words, and also that they were speaking of reconciling the two sisters, but they could find no way to get the elder to make peace. And the younger had agreed to abide by the King's decision and would not oppose it in any way. But the elder sister was so obstinate that even Queen Guinevere and those who knew their laws and the knights and the King were on the side of the younger; and everyone came to the King, begging that, despite the elder sister, he give the third or the fourth part of the land to the younger, and that he separate the two knights, for they both were of great valiance, and it would be too great a misfortune if one of them seriously wounded the other, or took away even the smallest part of his honor. And the King said that he would never intervene in making peace, because the elder sister was not interested in it, being such a completely evil creature.

All these words were heard by the two, who were wounding one another so that it was a great source of wonder for all; and the fight was so even that there was no way to tell who had the better and who the worse of it. And even the two who were fighting, and purchasing honor with suffering, marveled and were astonished that they were so equally matched, and each wondered mightily who this was who resisted him so fiercely. They went on fighting so long that day was drawing toward night; each of them had a tired arm and a pain-wracked body. And their blood was hotly boiling from their bodies in many places, and running under their hauberks; it is no wonder they wished to rest, for they were in great pain.

Then they both rested, and each thought to himself that he had now at long last met his match. They rested a long time, for they dared not resume fighting; they cared no more about the battle, both because of the coming darkness of the night and because they greatly feared each other. Both these things pushed them, and summoned them to remain at peace; but before leaving the field of battle they would know one another well, and there would be joy and pity between them.

My Lord Ywain, who was both very valiant and very courtly, spoke first, but to his misfortune his good friend failed to recognize him as he spoke, for his speech was low and his voice was hoarse, and weak, and broken, because his blood was all agitated by the blows he had received. "Sir," said he, "night is coming on; I think that we shall never incur blame nor reproach if night separates us. But I say this much: for my part I both fear and esteem you highly, and never in my life did I undertake a battle which caused me so much suffering, nor encounter a knight whom I so much desired to see and to meet. I can have the highest esteem for you, for I thought to see myself defeated. You truly know how to place your blows and use them to good advantage. No knight I ever met knew how to deal out so many blows; I would rather have received fewer than you have given me today. Your blows have completely stunned me."

"Upon my word," said my Lord Gawain, "you are not so stunned or weak, for I am just as much or more so, and if I, in turn, made your acquaintance, it would likely not displease me at all. If I have loaned you some of my wealth, you have certainly repaid me well, both principal and interest, for you were more generous in repayment than I was in taking. But however the matter may turn out, since you wish me to tell you by what name I am called, never shall my name be hidden from you: my name is Gawain, son of King Lot."

When Ywain heard this news, he was astonished, and extremely troubled, by anger and despair; he flung his bloody sword and his broken shield to the ground, dismounted from his horse, and said: "Oh, what a misfortune! We have fought this battle because of a terrible mistake, since we did not recognize one another, for I should never have done battle against you, had I recognized you but rather would have declared myself defeated before the first blow, I assure you."

"What," said my Lord Gawain, "who are you?" "I am Ywain, who loves you more than any man in the world for as far as it spreads in all directions, for you have always loved me and honored me in all courts. But I wish to make amends and honor you in this matter: I declare myself completely defeated." "You would do this for me?" said my Lord the gentle Gawain. "I should certainly be very presumptuous if I accepted this declaration. Never will this honor be mine, but rather yours; I cede it to you." "Oh, fair Sire, say no more, for that could not be; I can no longer hold myself up, I am so wounded and vanquished." "Truly, you strive for naught," said his friend and companion. "But I am vanquished and wounded, nor do I say anything by way of flattery, for there is no one in the world so unknown to me that I should not say the same thing to him rather than suffer any more of those blows of yours."

So speaking they dismounted; each put his arms around the other's neck, and they embraced, but they did not leave off talking for that, for each claimed he was defeated. This dispute never ceased until the King and his nobles came running from all sides, and saw them greeting one another, and they greatly desired to hear what this could be, and who these knights were who were showing one another such great joy. "My Lords," said the King, "tell us what has suddenly created this friendship and this accord between you, where all day I have seen such hatred and such discord."

"Sire," said my Lord Gawain, his nephew, "the misfortune and the calamity which resulted in this battle will never be kept from you. Since you are now stopped to hear and to learn about it, there will surely be someone who will tell you the truth of it. I, who am your nephew Gawain, did not recognize my companion, my Lord Ywain here, until he—thanks be to him!—as it pleased God, asked me my name. Each told the other his name; then we recognized each other after we had fought well together. We fought well together, and if we had gone on fighting a little longer, it would have gone badly for me, for, upon my soul, he would have killed me by his prowess, and because of the wrong of her who had sent me into battle. But I prefer that my friend defeat me at arms rather than kill me."

Then my Lord Ywain's blood ran all hot, and he said: "Dear, fair Lord, God help me, you are very wrong to say that; but may my Lord the King know that in this battle I am defeated and completely at the mercy of my opponent."

"No, I am!" "No, I am!" said each of them in turn. Both were so high-born and noble that each granted and gave the other the victory and the victor's crown, but neither of them was willing to take it; rather, each did his best to make the King, and all his people, believe that he was defeated and at the other's mercy.

But the King put an end to the dispute, when he had listened to them for some time, and what he heard greatly pleased him and also the fact that he saw that they had embraced one another. Yet they had grievously wounded one another in several places. "My Lords," said he, "there is great love between you; you make that clear when each of you says that he is defeated. But now leave the matter to me and I shall arrange it, I believe, so well that it will be to your honor and everyone will approve me in this."

Then both promised him that they would do as he wished, exactly as he would command. And the King said that he would justly and faithfully arbitrate the quarrel. "Where," said he, "is the maiden who expulsed her sister from her land, and deprived her of her inheritance by force and without pity?" "Sire," she answered, "here I am." "Are you? Then come here. I knew a long time ago that you were disinheriting her. Her rights will no longer be disputed, since you have admitted the truth to me. You must renounce any claim to her share." "Oh, my Lord and King, if I gave a silly and foolish reply, you must not take advantage of it. In God's name, Sire, do me no wrong! You are the King, and you must avoid injustice and error." "That is why," said the King, "I wish to restore your sister to her rights, for I never intended to commit an injustice. And you have clearly heard that your knight and hers have both left the final decision up to me; I shall certainly not tell you what you want to hear, for you are obviously in the wrong. Each says he is defeated on the field of battle, so much does each wish to honor the other. I do not need to dwell on that, since the matter is left to my judgement: either you will do exactly as I say, abandoning your unjust claim, or else I shall say that my nephew has been defeated in arms. Then it will be worse for you; but I should be reluctant to say so."

He had no intention of doing it, but he said that in order to see whether he could frighten her so much that she would give her sister back her share of the inheritance, out of fear, for he had clearly seen that she would relinquish no part of it for anything that he might say to her, if force or fear were lacking.

Because of what she feared, she said to him: "Fair Sire, now I must do what you wish, but it saddens my heart to do so; still I shall do it, even though it displeases me, and my sister will have what is rightfully hers. For her part of my inheritance I give her you yourself as a guarantee, so that she may be more sure of it." "Invest her with it on the spot," said the King, "and let her become your liege woman, and hold it from you; and love her as your liege, and let her love you as her lady and as her own sister." Thus the King led the matter until the maiden was invested with her land, and she thanked him for it. And the King said to his nephew, the brave and valiant knight, that he should allow his armor to be removed, and that my Lord Ywain, if he pleased, should let his be likewise taken off, for they could well do without it thenceforth. Then the knights were disarmed, and they kissed one another as equals.

And while they were embracing they saw the lion coming at a run, seeking his master. As soon as he saw him, he began to show great joy; then you would have seen people drawing back; even the boldest fled. "Stay," said my Lord Ywain, "everyone. Why do you flee? No one is chasing you; never fear that the lion you see coming will do you any harm; please take my word for this, for he is mine and I am his; we are companions together." Then all who had heard about the adventures of the lion, and of him and his companion, knew truly that it was none other who had killed the wicked giant. And my Lord Gawain said to him: "My Lord companion,

God help me, you have mightily humiliated me: I have evilly repaid you for the service you rendered me in killing the giant for my nephews and my niece. I have thought a lot about you for a long time, and for this I was preoccupied, for people said that between us two there was friendship and love. I have long thought of it, but in vain, for I could not remember, nor had I ever heard tell of, any knight that I knew, in any land where I had been, who was called by the sobriquet of 'the Knight of the Lion'." While they were speaking thus, their armor was removed, and the lion came quickly toward where his master was sitting. When he came before him, the lion showed him great joy, as well as any dumb beast can.

It was necessary to take them both to an infirmary or to a sickroom, for in order to heal their wounds they needed both doctor and plaster. The King, who held them both very dear, had them brought before him. A physician who knew more about medicine than any man was then summoned by King Arthur. And he strove to cure them until he healed their wounds as well and as quickly as he could. When he had cured them both, my Lord Ywain, who had irrevocably devoted his heart to Love, saw clearly that he could not stay there and that he would in the end die for Love, if his lady did not take pity on him, who was dying in this way. He decided that he would leave the court all alone and go attack his spring; and there he would cause so much lightning and so much wind and so much rain, that of necessity she would have to make peace with him, or else he would never cease tormenting the spring, and causing rain and wind.